W9-AQG-194

Dining In—Salt Lake City

COOKBOOK

A Collection of Gourmet Recipes for Complete Meals
from the Salt Lake City Area's Finest Restaurants

Larry R. Gerlach
and
Carole B. von Schmidt

PEANUT BUTTER PUBLISHING
SEATTLE, WASHINGTON

TITLES IN SERIES

Cover Photography: Fred Milkie
Editor: Elaine Lotzkar

Copyright © 1985 by Peanut Butter Publishing
911 Western Avenue, Suite 401 Maritime Building
Seattle, Washington 98104
All rights reserved. Printed in the United States of America

ISBN 0-89716-139-4

For the Beehive State Chefs Association,
in recognition of continuing efforts to enhance the quality
of dining in Utah.

PREFACE

When the authors arrived in Utah in 1968, restaurants in Salt Lake City lacked a tradition of fine dining. Then, in the early 1970's the number and variety of restaurants offering gourmet food increased dramatically. Of the twenty-one restaurants featured in this book, only four were founded before 1970; eleven opened after 1980. Leadership of the dramatic restaurant revolution has been provided by a group of talented chefs and restaurateurs, mostly young, who have brought to the community the culinary trends of the nation and the world. Basic momentum has been provided by the Salt Lake area dining public, which is demanding ever more from restaurants in terms of nutritious, quality food that is both well-prepared and artfully presented. Fresh seafood, unavailable in our inland community a decade ago, is now commonplace, as are cookware shops, speciality food stores, and cooking schools. The future for dining in Salt Lake City is bright. For all the recent gastronomic developments, the area has only just begun to realize its culinary potential.

Dining out in Utah is complicated by the state liquor laws. Because Utah is a control state, persons wishing to enjoy alcoholic beverages with their meals have three options. First, one may bring to the restaurant liquor or wine purchased at a state liquor store—"brown bagging" in the local vernacular. The wine store in Trolley Square deserves special attention for premium domestic and international wines. Second, one may purchase alcoholic beverages at a restaurant which has a state liquor license; however, the selection varies and is restricted to minibottles of liquor and tenths of wine. A nominal fee is charged for set-ups or corkage. Third, one may join a private club which serves mixed drinks and wine without restriction. Two-week memberships are available for the state required fee of $5.00. Although the liquor laws are cumbersome, they need not interfere unduly with one's dining experiences.

The menus contained in this cookbook and restaurant guide demonstrate the quality and diversity of dining in Salt Lake City and the adjacent ski areas. Each recipe is kitchen tested to ensure accuracy. The authors owe a deep debt of gratitude to the chefs and restaurateurs who took time out from busy schedules to share their kitchens, recipes, and culinary expertise.

Larry R. Gerlach
Carole B. von Schmidt

CONTENTS

ADOLPH'S

Dinner for Four

Raclette Swiss Style

Garden Salad with Adolph's House Dressing

Veal Steak Madagascar

Swiss Rösti Potatoes

Carrots in Honey Sauce,   Cauliflower Maison,
and
Italian Squash with Dill

Strawberry Flambé with Vanilla Ice Cream

Wine:

Rutherford Hill, Jaeger Vineyards, Chardonnay, 1981
or
Monmousseau Vouvray, 1983

Adolph Imboden, Owner-Chef

A dolph Imboden has a natural affinity for both the kitchen and the ski slope. As a youngster in Interlaken, Switzerland, he grew up skiing and helping his parents operate their hotel and restaurant. After graduating from the Swiss Hotel Management School *Montana* in Lucerne, he always found a way to combine his love of skiing and cooking. A certified advanced ski instructor in Switzerland and the United States, Adolph's culinary career unfolded in places with names like St. Moritz, Lake Tahoe, and Vail. He came to Park City in 1971, and three years later opened his own restaurant adjacent to the golf course.

Although Adolph still races competitively "to keep active and maintain balance in life," he is best known to Utahns as a chef. Quality and consistency are the trademarks of Adolph's. "I like to offer new things, but still keep the kind of food on the menu that people seem to enjoy so much." The speciality of the house is veal, particularly Veal Adolph, a classic presentation of minced veal in a mushroom and cream sauce served over noodles. "I'm very much into simplified, healthful food. I am a great admirer of Paul Bocuse, perhaps the greatest living chef." Adolph's treatment of vegetables exemplifies his belief in cooking as "a culinary art." "Vegetables are not often done very well, but we try to do them properly—always just done with the right seasonings."

The decor is quintessential alpine resort. Wood and windows dominate the dining room, from the exposed ceiling beam trusses to the wraparound picture windows that provide an unobstructed view of the mountains and ski slopes. Numerous lush green plants provide an element of serenity, but the pictures, posters, and the display of skiing trophies won by Adolph and his employees in individual or team competition carry out the dominant theme of dynamic outdoor activity. The atmosphere may be casual and relaxed, but the formal table settings and crisply efficient service are indicative of a first-class restaurant.

"Atmosphere, service, and quality food is the combination for success in the restaurant business," maintains Adolph. Judging from its longstanding popularity, Adolph's has mastered all three elements.

1541 Thaynes Canyon Drive   649-4277
Park City

RACLETTE SWISS STYLE

1 pound imported Raclette cheese
4 French cornichons or
 baby dill pickles, diced
4 small new potatoes,
 boiled and peeled

4 tomato wedges
12 pearl onions
 Paprika

1. Cut the Raclette cheese into very thin slices. Divide the slices among 4 oven-proof plates.
2. Place the plates under a broiler until the cheese melts and begins to brown, about 4 minutes.
3. Garnish each plate with a diced pickle, potato, tomato wedge, 3 pearl onions, and a dash of paprika. Serve immediately.

Raclette, a specialty of the Swiss canton of Valais, is available in any good cheese shop. This dish is a variety of Swiss cheese fondue.

GARDEN SALAD WITH ADOLPH'S HOUSE DRESSING

½ head iceberg lettuce
½ head red leaf lettuce
1 head Boston Bibb lettuce
1 large tomato, sliced

1 large cucumber, peeled, seeded, and sliced
4 mushrooms, sliced
1 basket alfalfa sprouts
ADOLPH'S HOUSE DRESSING

1. Wash and dry the lettuce.

2. Tear the iceberg and red leaf lettuce into bite-size pieces. Arrange the Bibb lettuce leaves on chilled salad plates. Add a mixture of iceberg and red leaf lettuce pieces. Garnish with the tomato, cucumber, mushrooms, and alfalfa sprouts. Top with ADOLPH'S HOUSE DRESSING.

ADOLPH'S HOUSE DRESSING

2 egg yolks
1 clove garlic, finely chopped
2 teaspoons finely chopped onion
1 tablespoon Worcestershire sauce
1 tablespoon Dijon mustard
2 tablespoons mayonnaise
Juice of ½ lemon

1 tablespoon red wine vinegar
1 tablespoon brandy
1 tablespoon light cream (half and half)
½-⅔ cup salad oil
Salt and pepper to taste
1-2 teaspoons fresh dill or 1 teaspoon dried dill

1. In a large mixing bowl, whisk together the egg yolks, garlic, onion, Worcestershire, mustard and mayonnaise until well blended. Add the lemon juice, vinegar, brandy, and cream. Whisk until combined.

2. Slowly add the salad oil, whisking constantly, until the dressing reaches a smooth and creamy consistency. Add salt and pepper to taste.

3. Stir in the fresh dill just before serving.

VEAL STEAK MADAGASCAR

4 (6-7 ounce) veal steaks,
    cut from the loin
    Salt and white pepper
1 tablespoon chopped fresh basil
    mixed with olive oil
    to form a pesto
    Flour
1 tablespoon butter
1 tablespoon oil

1 tablespoon brandy
1 tablespoon Dijon mustard
1 tablespoon green peppercorns
1 tablespoon finely chopped
    shallots
1 cup veal stock (see index)
½ cup heavy cream
⅓ cup dry white wine
    Chopped parsley

1. Sprinkle the veal steaks with salt and white pepper. Rub lightly with the basil pesto. Dredge lightly in the flour, shaking off any excess flour.

2. Melt the butter with the oil in a skillet over high heat. Add the veal and brown on both sides. Lower the heat to medium and cook until desired doneness, about 8 minutes in all for medium. Sprinkle the veal with the brandy and ignite. When the flame dies out, remove the veal to a platter and keep warm.

3. Remove the skillet from the heat. Add to the cooking juices and butter the mustard, peppercorns, and shallots. Return to medium heat and sauté 1 minute, stirring frequently. Add the veal stock, cream, and white wine. Let reduce until the liquid reaches a thickened, creamy consistency. It should be pourable but not runny. Add any juices released by the reserved veal steaks. Season with salt and white pepper to taste. Return the veal steaks to the sauce, turn to coat, and warm for 30 seconds.

4. Transfer the veal steaks to serving plates. Top with the sauce. Sprinkle with chopped parsley.

Adolph's serves veal steaks with the bone in, trimmed French style as for a rack of lamb. Any cut of veal will do, as it is the green pepper sauce that makes the dish.

SWISS RÖSTI POTATOES

4-5 *large new potatoes*
  2 *tablespoons butter*
  2 *slices bacon,*
     cut into small pieces

½ *small onion, finely chopped*
  Salt and white pepper
1 *tablespoon butter,*
  cut into small pieces
  Chopped parsley

1. Boil the potatoes until just tender. Cool, peel, and shred into large strips.
2. In a large skillet, melt the butter over medium heat. Add ½ of the bacon pieces and ½ of the chopped onion. Sauté for 1 minute. Add the shredded potatoes. Sprinkle liberally with salt and white pepper. Top with the remaining bacon and onion. Cook until the bottom of the potato patty is golden brown, 5 to 6 minutes.
3. Invert the potato patty onto a buttered plate. Add additional butter to the skillet if necessary. Slide the potato patty carefully back into the skillet, uncooked side down, and sauté until the bottom is golden brown, 5 to 6 minutes. Just before the potatoes are done, distribute butter pieces over the top of the patty.
4. Transfer the potato patty to a round serving platter. Sprinkle with the parsley. Divide into pie-shaped serving pieces at the table.

Although skillets with non-stick surfaces are not recommended for browning meats and sautéing in general, they are wonderful for cooking potatoes and eggs. They are highly recommended additions to any well-equipped kitchen.

CARROTS IN HONEY SAUCE

4 medium carrots
1 tablespoon butter
2 tablespoons honey

1 tablespoon brown sugar
Swiss Knorr Aromat

1. Peel the carrots and cut into julienne strips of preferred length and thickness. Blanch in boiling water until crisp-tender. Drain.
2. Melt the butter in a skillet. Stir in the honey and brown sugar. Add the carrots and sprinkle with Swiss Knorr Aromat. Toss the carrots gently to cover with the sauce and cook to desired tenderness.

Swiss Knorr Aromat, available in most supermarkets, is an excellent blend of spices used for seasoning vegetables and seafood.

CAULIFLOWER MAISON

8 medium or 4 large
    cauliflower florets
1 tablespoon butter

½ teaspoon lemon juice
¼ cup bread crumbs
½ teaspoon chopped parsley

1. Blanch the cauliflower florets in boiling water to desired doneness, about 5 minutes.
2. Melt the butter in a small saucepan, stir in the lemon juice, bread crumbs, and parsley. Add additional butter or bread crumbs as needed.
3. Serve the cauliflower florets topped with the hot bread crumb mixture.

ITALIAN SQUASH WITH DILL

1 zucchini squash
1 yellow banana squash
1 tablespoon butter
1 teaspoon finely chopped
   shallots
¼ teaspoon finely chopped garlic

2 teaspoons chopped tomato
⅛ teaspoon chopped parsley
2 tablespoons dry white wine
  Salt and white pepper
  Swiss Knorr Aromat
1-2 teaspoons fresh dill

1. Using a stripper or scorer, remove strips of peeling from the squash lengthwise at regular intervals. Cut into ⅛-inch slices.

2. Melt the butter in a skillet. Add the shallots and garlic. Sauté for 30 seconds. Add the tomato, parsley, and white wine. Stir. Add the squash slices and sprinkle with salt, white pepper, and Swiss Knorr Aromat. Sauté briefly until crisp-tender. Sprinkle with fresh dill to taste.

STRAWBERRY FLAMBÉ WITH VANILLA ICE CREAM

2 tablespoons butter
1 tablespoon sugar
1 tablespoon honey
 Juice of ½ lemon
 Juice of ½ orange
1 tablespoon Triple Sec liqueur

1 pint fresh strawberries,
 stemmed and halved
1 tablespoon 151-proof rum
 or brandy
4 large scoops vanilla ice cream,
 home-made or Häagen-Dazs
4 fresh mint leaves

1. Melt the butter in a skillet over medium heat. Add the sugar, honey, lemon juice, and orange juice. Cook until the ingredients are well blended and form a light syrup.

2. Add the Triple Sec and strawberries. Sauté until the berries are softened and warmed through. Add the rum or brandy and ignite. Cook until the liquid is reduced to desired consistency.

3. Spoon the strawberry sauce over the ice cream. Garnish with a mint leaf.

This recipe can easily be doubled. Other fruit may be substituted for the strawberries. If using raspberries, substitute Framboise, Kirsch, or Creme de Cassis for the Triple Sec. If peaches are used, substitute Amaretto for the Triple Sec.

Alta Lodge

Dinner for Six

Mushrooms à la Grecque

Curry Vegetable Soup

Green Salad with Vinaigrette Dressing

Tournedos with Sauce Raddon

Asparagus with Sauce Hollandaise

Poppy Seed Bread

Almond Cake

Wine:

With the Tournedos—Pine Ridge Cabernet Sauvignon, 1981

William Levitt, Owner
Bino Levitt, Manager
Paul Raddon, Chef
Rob Landis, Sous Chef
Donna Holt, Baker

Located at the head of Little Cottonwood Canyon some 26 miles from Salt Lake City, the recently incorporated village of Alta, once a booming mining town, is a haven for visitors drawn by "the greatest snow on earth" in the winter and the alpine beauty of the Wasatch National Forest in the summer. The focal point of the tiny town is the historic Alta Lodge, built in 1940 to service one of the first chairlifts in the West. The venerable lodge has undergone extensive expansion in facilities and services since acquired in 1959 by William Levitt, a native of New York City who "fell in love with the place" while on a ski vacation. Rated "Exceptional" by the AAA, the lodge ranks among the premier mountain inns in America.

The Alta Lodge prides itself on serving "world renowned cuisine in a mountain setting." From the simple elegance of the winter menu to the international cuisine offered in the summer dining room, Chef Paul Raddon since 1969 has maintained a tradition of gourmet dining. "As a resort hotel, we attract people from all over the world. Our guests have diverse tastes and discriminating palates, so it becomes quite a challenge to prepare a variety of foods to meet their expectations." Raddon meets the challenge in part by having fresh produce and seafood flown in throughout the year and by making extensive use of unusual and sophisticated sauces to complement entrées. The bakery staff is justifiably proud of its handiwork, especially the popular chocolate soufflé, an ethereal concoction painstakingly developed for an altitude of 8,600 feet.

Guests and the general public are offered a choice of four entrées during the ski season and a full menu during the summer. Vegetarian meals are available at all times, and a special Sunday brunch is prepared during the summer. For a bonus, the wall-wide picture window in the dining room affords a spectacular view down the granite-faced, glacial canyon toward the setting sun.

Alta, Utah   742-3500

MUSHROOMS À LA GRECQUE

1½ cups chicken broth
1½ cups dry white wine
⅓ cup olive oil
⅓ cup lemon juice
¾ teaspoon salt
2 large shallots, minced
1 large clove garlic, minced
5 sprigs parsley
1 tablespoon dried cardamom

½ teaspoon thyme
1 large bay leaf
1½ pounds small mushrooms, cleaned, stems removed, and fluted
4 tablespoons parsley, finely minced
4 large lettuce leaves, Bibb or red leaf

1. Combine all ingredients except the mushrooms, minced parsley and lettuce in a medium saucepan. Bring to a boil, reduce heat, and simmer for 30 minutes.

2. Strain the mixture through a fine sieve. Discard the solids and return the liquid to the saucepan. Add the mushrooms and simmer for 10 minutes. Transfer the mushrooms with a slotted spoon to a ceramic or glass bowl and set aside.

3. Reduce the cooking liquid over high heat to 1 cup. Pour the liquid over the mushrooms and marinate, covered, in the refrigerator for at least 4 hours.

4. To serve, arrange the mushrooms on Bibb or red leaf lettuce on chilled serving plates, spoon some of the marinade over each serving, and sprinkle with minced parsley.

CURRY VEGETABLE SOUP

5 cups chicken stock	1 teaspoon turmeric
2 cups coarsely chopped carrots	3½ cups half and half
2 medium potatoes, peeled and quartered	Salt and pepper to taste
2 cups peas	¼ cup carrots, julienne cut and blanched until tender
2½ cups coarsely chopped broccoli	¼ cup zucchini, julienne cut and blanched until tender
6 tablespoons olive oil	¼ cup finely chopped parsley
1 cup diced onion	
1½ tablespoons curry powder	

1. In a large saucepot or kettle, bring the chicken stock, carrots, potatoes, peas, and broccoli to a boil. Reduce the heat and simmer until the carrots and potatoes are soft, about 15 minutes. Remove from heat and allow to cool.

2. In a skillet, heat the olive oil over medium heat and sauté the onions with the curry powder and turmeric until the onions are soft.

3. Add the onions and the half and half to the stock. Blend well. Add salt and pepper to taste. Pass the soup through a sieve, pressing the solids with the back of a wooden spoon or a spatula. If the soup seems too thick, add more half and half. Adjust seasonings.

4. Serve piping hot, garnished with carrot and zucchini julienne and the chopped parsley.

A savory soup is essential throughout the year. In the summer we feature light soups that emphasize fresh fruits and vegetables—Gazpacho, Fresh Tomato Broth, and Blueberry Yogurt Soup are favorites. In the winter hearty creamed soups are featured. The most popular winter soup is Curry Vegetable, our adaptation of Mulligatawny, the classic curry soup of India.

GREEN SALAD WITH VINAIGRETTE DRESSING

1 *head Boston lettuce*
1 *head red leaf lettuce*

Radicchio
1 *small Belgian endive*
   VINAIGRETTE DRESSING

Wash the lettuce, tear into pieces, and dry. Arrange the lettuce on a plate with a few pieces of radicchio and endive for accent. Top with VINAIGRETTE DRESSING.

VINAIGRETTE DRESSING

2-3 *shallots, finely minced*
 ½ *teaspoon dry mustard*
1½ *tablespoons red wine vinegar*
 1 *tablespoon fresh lemon juice*

 ½ *cup olive*
 ¼ *teaspoon salt or to taste*
   Fresh ground black pepper
    to taste
 ¼ *teaspoon dried tarragon*

Blend all ingredients.

TOURNEDOS with SAUCE RADDON

3 *pounds beef tenderloin*   *SAUCE RADDON*

1. Slice the tenderloin into 12 filets, 4 ounces each (about ½-inch thick). Grill or pan fry the filets to desired doneness.
2. Serve 2 filets per person placed on a thin layer of SAUCE RADDON.

SAUCE RADDON

2 *tablespoons butter*
3 *small shallots, diced*
2 *cups beef consommé*
   (canned is acceptable)
½ *cup dry red wine*

½ *cup ruby port*
¼ *cup Major Grey's Chutney*
   (Indian Mango)
1 *teaspoon Dijon mustard*
4 *tablespoons tomato paste*

1. Melt the butter over medium heat and sauté the shallots until translucent. Reserve.
2. In a saucepan reduce the consommé over medium high heat to 1 cup. Add the red wine, the port, and the shallots and reduce to 1 cup. Strain out the shallots. Reserve the liquid.
3. Process the chutney in a blender adding enough water, about 2 tablespoons, to make a smooth sauce. Pass through a fine strainer.
4. Over medium heat, cook the consommé-wine liquid, chutney, mustard, and tomato paste until the mixture becomes thick enough to coat lightly the back of a spoon.

ASPARAGUS with SAUCE HOLLANDAISE

12-18 large spears asparagus,   *SAUCE HOLLANDAISE*
        trimmed and scraped

1. Cook the asparagus spears in a steamer or in boiling, salted water until just tender, 10 to 12 minutes.
2. Serve with SAUCE HOLLANDAISE.

SAUCE HOLLANDAISE

   6 *egg yolks*   *Salt and white pepper to taste*
   ½ *pound butter, cut into*   3 *teaspoons lemon juice or to taste*
       tablespoon-sized chunks   3 *teaspoons warm water*

1. Place the egg yolks in the top of a double boiler and whisk briskly over simmering but not boiling water.
2. When the eggs are hot to the touch, add the butter, a few tablespoons at a time, whisking constantly.
3. Add the salt, white pepper, and lemon juice, 1 teaspoon at a time, to taste. Whisk in the warm water, 1 teaspoon at a time, to thin the sauce if necessary. Use SAUCE HOLLANDAISE at once.

An asparagus cooker can be improvised by punching holes in the bottom of a 46-ounce juice can. Stand the asparagus spears in the can and place in a pot of boiling water. The boiling water should come within 1 inch or so of the asparagus tips so that the tender tips steam while the tougher stalks par boil.

POPPY SEED BREAD

1¼ cups milk
⅔ cup butter or margarine,
    room temperature
½ cup plus 1 teaspoon sugar
2 teaspoons salt
2 packages dry yeast
½ cup warm water (105-115°)

2 eggs, beaten,
    at room temperature
5 cups all-purpose flour
    (approximately)
1 egg beaten with 1 teaspoon
    water for glaze
Poppy seeds as needed

1. Scald the milk. Pour it over the butter or margarine, ½ cup sugar, and salt in a large mixing bowl. Mix well and let cool to lukewarm.

2. Dissolve the yeast in the warm water with 1 teaspoon sugar. Let proof 3 to 4 minutes.

3. Add the yeast and eggs to the milk mixture. Mix well. Stir in 2 cups of flour. Gradually add additional flour, ½ cup at a time, to make a rough mass that cleans the sides of the bowl.

4. Turn the dough onto a floured work surface and knead until smooth and elastic, about 8 minutes. Add additional flour if the dough seems too sticky.

5. Place the dough in a lightly buttered bowl, turning once to coat the surface with a film of butter. Cover the bowl with plastic wrap and let rise in a warm place (80-85°) until doubled in bulk, about 1 hour.

6. Punch down the dough, return to the work surface, and knead gently for 30 seconds to remove air bubbles. Divide the dough in half. Shape into 2 loaves and place in 2 9x5-inch greased loaf pans, or shape into either 2 round loaves or 2 braided loaves and place on a greased baking sheet. Cover with wax paper and return to the warm place until the dough has doubled in bulk, about 1 hour.

7. Preheat the oven to 375° for metal, 350° for glass pans. Brush the loaves with the egg wash and sprinkle liberally with poppy seeds. Bake for approximately 30 minutes until the tops are golden brown and the loaves sound hollow when tapped on the bottom. Cool on a metal rack.

ALMOND CAKE

¼ pound unsalted butter,
  room temperature
½ cup sugar
10 ounces almond paste
3 eggs, unbeaten,
  at room temperature

¼ teaspoon salt
2½ tablespoons flour
2½ tablespoons Kirsch
  Powdered sugar as needed
  Berry purée (optional)

1. Preheat the oven to 325°.

2. Grease an 8-inch springform cake pan. Cut parchment paper to fit the bottom of the pan. Grease and flour the parchment paper and sides of the pan. Set aside.

3. In an electric mixer, cream the butter and sugar until very smooth, 8 to 10 minutes.

4. Add the almond paste and beat until very well blended.

5. Add the eggs to the batter, one at a time, mixing thoroughly before adding the next egg.

6. Add the salt, flour, and Kirsch. Blend well.

7. Pour the batter into the prepared cake pan. Distribute and smooth the batter with a spatula.

8. Bake on the middle rack of a 325° oven for approximately 50 minutes. The cake is done when the sides pull away from the pan, the top is firm, and a toothpick inserted into the center of the cake comes out clean. Let the cake rest 4 to 5 minutes before removing from the pan.

9. Just before serving, dust the top of the cake with powdered sugar. A dollop of fresh berry purée, especially raspberry, makes a delicious accompaniment.

Parchment paper is essential to prevent sticking. The almond paste must be added before the eggs or the mixture will not blend well. Unsalted butter must be used to produce maximum results. Because the cake contains no leavening agent, the cake will rise only slightly and have a delicate, moist, granular texture; no adjustments for altitude are necessary.

B I R D ' S   C A F E

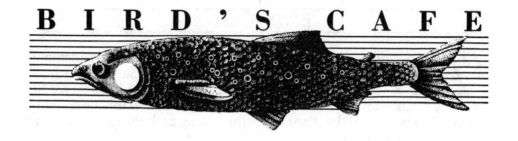

Dinner for Four

Fettuccine with Bay Scallops

Bird's Special Salad

Breast of Chicken Jerusalem

Carrots Vichy

Lemon Mousse

Wines:

With the Fettuccine and Chicken—Eyrie Pinot Gris, 1982

With the Mousse—Korbel Extra Dry Sparkling Wine

Dennis C. Bird, Owner-Chef

"An American grill" is how Denny Bird describes his restaurant. "I love San Francisco grills, especially Sam's, and hope Bird's Cafe plays that kind of role here." It does, for his intimate establishment is always crowded for lunch, and the dinner hour often extends far into the night as patrons enjoy both the good food and the relaxed atmosphere.

Chef Bird describes his style of cooking as "very simple·" "This is my home town, and I know that the community wants wholesome, understandable food with a special touch." Usually, the "special touch" is provided by one of his light and flavorful sauces. "A good kitchen revolves around the stock pot," he confides. The regular menu is brief. Customers instinctively turn to the large blackboards for the daily listing of fish, seafood, pasta, and dessert specials. There are always at least two Blue Plate Specials.

Although Bird jokingly refers to the interior design of the restaurant as "a mish-mash that works," the truth is that his wife, Linda, a designer, developed a stiking decor that effectively matches the cuisine. The black and white tile floors, long wooden bar, brass rails, wood chairs, and green and black vinyl tablecloths provide an invitingly unpretentious atmosphere. Everything about Bird's is straightforward and personal. The seemingly eclectic collection of photographs, certificates, posters, and pictures that adorn the wall are actually treasured mementos representing special events in Bird's life. In effect, the restaurant is Bird's home, the dining room the den into which he welcomes friends old and new.

59 East 1700 South   466-1051
Salt Lake City

FETTUCCINE WITH BAY SCALLOPS

10 ounces fettuccine noodles,
  (De Cecco brand, if packaged)
3 tablespoons olive oil
2 tablespoons butter
6 ounces bay scallops
¾ cup clam juice

1 cup heavy (whipping) cream
3 tablespoons grated Parmesan
  cheese
Fresh ground pepper to taste
2 tablespoons chopped parsley
4 lemon wedges

1. Plunge the noodles into a pot of boiling, salted water with the olive oil. Cook until *al dente*. Remove from the heat and let the noodles swell for 5 minutes in the hot water. Rinse the noodles in cold water to stop the cooking and remove excess starch. Drain and reserve.

2. Melt the butter over medium heat in a large skillet. Sauté the scallops for 30 seconds. Add the clam juice, cream, and cheese. Stir to incorporate. Add the reserved noodles and cook until the sauce is thickened and reduced, 5 to 6 minutes. Add fresh ground pepper to taste. Stir in the parsley.

3. Serve on warmed plates with a lemon wedge for garnish.

For variation, substitute clams or mussels for the scallops.

BIRD'S SPECIAL SALAD

6 ounces fresh green beans
½ small head of lettuce, washed dried, torn in bite-size pieces
2 canned hearts of palm, cut into ½-inch pieces
4 canned artichoke hearts, halved
2 medium tomatoes, cut into ¾-inch dice

1 cucumber, peeled and cut into ¾-inch dice
2 green onions, chopped
16 ripe black olives, quartered
2 tablespoons fresh chopped parsley
VINAIGRETTE DRESSING

1. Blanch the green beans in boiling water until crisp-tender, 6 to 7 minutes. Refresh in cold water. Cut into 2-inch lengths.
2. Combine the green beans with the other vegetables. Toss with the VINAIGRETTE DRESSING. Serve on chilled plates.

VINAIGRETTE DRESSING

¼ cup red wine vinegar
¾ cup olive oil

1 tablespoon Dijon mustard
Salt and fresh ground black pepper to taste

Thoroughly blend the vinegar, olive oil, and mustard. Add salt and pepper to taste.

BREAST OF CHICKEN JERUSALEM

4 *whole chicken breasts, boned*	1 *cup mushroom slices*
Salt	4 *canned artichokes, quartered*
White pepper	16 *ripe black olives, pitted*
Nutmeg	1 *tablespoon lemon juice*
Flour	1 *cup dry sherry*
4 *tablespoons butter*	1½ *cups chicken stock*
2 *tablespoons finely chopped*	½ *cup heavy (whipping) cream*
shallots	2 *tablespoons chopped parsley*

1. Sprinkle the chicken breasts, skin side only, with salt, pepper, and nutmeg. Dredge in flour. Melt the butter in a large skillet over medium heat. Sauté the chicken breasts, skin side down, 3 to 4 minutes. Turn the breasts and add the shallots, mushrooms, artichokes, olives, and lemon juice. Cook 2 minutes. Add the sherry. Cover and simmer until most of the liquid is absorbed, about 5 minutes. Add the chicken stock and cream. Simmer, covered, 15 to 20 minutes. If the sauce seems too thick, add up to ½ cup more chicken stock. Adjust the seasoning. Sprinkle with the chopped parsley.

2. Divide the chicken breasts among four serving plates. Serve with CARROTS VICHY.

The small amount of chicken stock required for this recipe can be made by boning the breasts ahead of time and then simmering the bones for 2 to 3 hours in 3 cups of water with a rough cut carrot, a coarsely chopped celery stalk, ¼ onion, and a small bouquet garni.

This is a classic dish that I've been doing for years. I keep thinking about changing it or dropping it from the menu, but so many people come here for it that I wouldn't dare do anything to it. It's the most popular item on the menu.

CARROTS VICHY

2 medium carrots,
   peeled and sliced
¼ cup chopped onion
1 tablespoon chopped parsley

4 tablespoons butter
1 cup 7-Up
1 cup club soda
   Salt and white pepper to taste

1. Sauté the carrots, onion, and parsley in the butter until the carrots are about half cooked, 6 to 8 minutes. Adjust the heat so that the carrots and onions do not brown.

2. Add 7-Up and club soda. Cook, uncovered, over medium heat until the carrots are just tender and the liquid has almost evaporated. Add the salt and white pepper to taste.

Traditionally, this dish called for vichy water and brown sugar. Club soda and 7-up are a good substitute. Use 2 cups of 7-Up for a sweeter taste.

LEMON MOUSSE

4 *egg yolks, room temperature*
½ *cup sugar*
½ *cup lemon juice*
  Grated rind of 1 lemon

2 *cups heavy (whipping) cream*
  Lemon zest for garnish
4 *whole strawberries for garnish*
4 *mint leaves for garnish*

1. Combine the egg yolks, sugar, lemon juice, and grated lemon rind in a stainless steel bowl. Place the bowl on top of a pot of boiling water and beat with a wire whisk or electric hand mixer until the mixture forms soft peaks, 5 to 6 minutes. Remove from the heat and continue beating for another 3 minutes. Set aside to cool for 10 minutes.

2. In another bowl, beat the cream until it forms stiff peaks. Using a rubber spatula, gently fold the whipped cream into the egg mixture. Spoon the mousse into dessert goblets. Chill.

3. Serve the Lemon Mousse garnished with strips of lemon zest, a strawberry, and a mint leaf.

This is a simple dessert so long as the heat is controlled. It is important to cook the egg mixture in a make-shift double boiler to reduce the heat and thus avoid making scrambled eggs. It is also important that the egg mixture cools to lukewarm before folding in the whipped cream to avoid the cream breaking down.

C·A·F·E
MARIPOSA

Dinner for Six

Vegetable Terrine Girardet

Scallop Provençal Soup

Fettuccine with Morels and Sweetbreads

Roast Squab with Port Wine Sauce and Wild Rice

Floating Islands with Orange Sauce

Wines:
With the Terrine—Perrier Jouet Grand Brut
With the Soup—Guigal Hermitage Blanc, 1978
With the Fettuccine—St. Clement Sauvignon Blanc, 1982
With the Squab—Stag's Leap Merlot, 1980
With the Floating Islands—Chateau St. Jean Select Private Reserve, 1982

William J. Nassikas, Director of Food and Beverage, Deer Valley Resort
Franklin Biggs, Executive Chef, Silver Lake Lodge
Peter Leonard, Chef, Cafe Mariposa

CAFE MARIPOSA

At Deer Valley, the acknowledged state-of-the-art luxury ski resort adjacent to Park City, as much emphasis is placed on gourmet food as on grand skiing. The culinary jewel of the resort complex is the Cafe Mariposa, located in the Silver Lake day lodge at the base of Bald Mountain. Cafe Mariposa was established to serve light lunches to skiers, but under the direction of William J. Nassikas, brilliant hotelier, and Franklin Biggs, named to *Food & Wine* magazine's Honor Roll of American Chefs, has become a premier full-service restaurant.

As indicated by the selection of the name Mariposa (Spanish for lily, in recognition of Utah's state flower, the sego lily), the watchwords of the restaurant are simplicity, subtlety, and attention to detail. An atmosphere of dignified ruggedness and informal elegance suggested by the visual unity of the redwood paneled walls, the massive stone fireplace, the charming antiques, and the oak tables and chairs is confirmed by the delicate fresh Ulstrameria lilies that grace tables throughout the year.

Executive Chef Biggs, who trained at La Varenne and apprenticed at Maxim's and Taillevent in Paris, describes the cuisine as "electic, neither French nor American. Instead, we use the culinary traditions of Europe to enhance the natural qualities of American products. We seek out the best and freshest products and treat them simply in preparation and presentation." The menu is limited by design. "By limiting the quantity of what we do, we can focus on the quality of what we do. Everything that goes onto a plate must be the very best it can possibly be. We demand the best of our purveyors, the best of our kitchen staff, and the best of our service personnel. And we even like to demand the best of our guests—if something isn't right, we want to know about it."

It is the unqualified commitment to quality and painstaking attention to detail that enables the Cafe Mariposa to promise patrons a superlative dining experience—and to exceed expectations.

Silver Lake Lodge   649-1000
Deer Valley

VEGETABLE TERRINE GIRARDET

1 *pound carrots, cut into*
⅛-inch brunoise (dice)
1 *pound turnips, cut into*
⅛-inch brunoise (dice)
½ *pound broccoli, trimmed into*
small florets
12 *ounces parsley, trimmed of*
most stems
½ *pound chicken breast, poached,*
skinned, and boned

1 *cup heavy (whipping) cream*
Salt and white pepper to taste
1 *fresh foie gras (1 pound*
approximately), soaked
1 hour in tepid water
HAZELNUT-SHERRY
VINAIGRETTE
4-5 *tablespoons hazelnuts,*
roasted and chopped
1 *tomato, peeled, seeded, and cut*
into ⅛-inch brunoise (dice)

1. Blanch the carrots, turnips, and broccoli separately in boiling water until only slightly firm. Refresh in cold water and spread on a towel to dry. Blanch the parsley until well cooked, about 8 minutes; refresh in cold water to retain green color, and squeeze very dry with your hands.

2. Purée the parsley and chicken in a food processor to a very smooth consistency. Force the purée through a drum sieve (tamis) to produce a fine purée. Place the purée in a bowl set in ice and beat in the cream, about 2 tablespoons at a time. Stir in 1 teaspoon of salt and ½ teaspoon pepper or to taste. Make sure the purée is well seasoned.

3. Devein the foie gras if necessary, making as few cuts as possible, and remove any skin. Slice the foie gras on the bias into slices ½-inch thick.

4. Butter a 1½-liter rectangular terrine mold. Line the mold with aluminum foil, dull side facing in, and butter the foil.

5. Smooth a little of the purée in the bottom of the mold making a thin, uniform layer about ⅛-inch thick. Mix the rest of the purée with the carrots, turnips, and broccoli. Fill the mold to almost ½ full. Bang the mold firmly on a hard surface to remove any air bubbles and to set the purée. Layer the foie gras, using the largest possible pieces, and press down to get as uniform a layer as possible. Spread the rest of the purée-vegetable mixture on top of the foie gras layer and fill the mold. Do not worry if the mixture mounds over the top of the mold as it will shrink as it cooks.

continued…

6. Place a lid of buttered wax paper on top of the mold. Place the mold in a water bath with a towel on the bottom to protect the terrine from direct heat. Fill with water to a level about ¾ up the side of the mold. Cook in an oven for 35 to 40 minutes at 325°. Refrigerate for 24 hours before serving.

7. To serve, remove the wax paper from the top of the terrine and unmold by dipping briefly in hot water and inverting on a platter. Spoon a thin layer of HAZELNUT-SHERRY VINAIGRETTE on each plate. Sprinkle with toasted hazelnuts and the tomato brunoise. Serve each person a ¼-inch thick slice of terrine; spread the top with a thin layer of VINAIGRETTE.

HAZELNUT-SHERRY VINAIGRETTE

¾ cup hazelnut oil   Salt and white pepper to taste
¼ cup sherry

Blend well all ingredients.

Fresh foie gras, available at speciality markets, makes the terrine an elegant, sumptuous dish. If unavailable, omit entirely as there is no acceptable sustitute for foie gras.

The success of this dish depends on attention to detail and taking the extra steps necessary to produce a superior product. The parsley must be cooked until very tender or it will not purée properly. The parsley and chicken must be processed until reaching a very smooth consistency or the mixture will not pass through the sieve. The use of a tamis instead of a fine strainer is more effort, but the extra fine purée is well worth the effort. Cutting vegetables into ⅛-inch brunoise is tedious, but gives the terrine a memorable texture. Beating the cream into the purée over ice promotes stability; if the mixture becomes warm, the cream will not incorporate properly.

SCALLOP PROVENÇAL SOUP

1 bunch basil
  (approximately ½ ounce)
  Olive oil
1 medium onion, chopped
1 bulb fennel, chopped
4 cloves garlic, finely chopped
1 tablespoon olive oil
1 cup white wine

¼ cup Pernod
5 cups FISH STOCK
4 medium tomatoes, peeled,
  seeded, and chopped into
  ¼-inch pieces
1 teaspoon tomato paste (optional)
1 pound bay scallops
  Salt and white pepper to taste

1. In a blender, combine the basil with enough olive oil to make a smooth paste (pesto). Reserve 2 tablespoons of the pesto for garnish.

2. In a medium saucepot, sauté the onion, fennel, garlic, and pesto in the 1 tablespoon olive oil over medium heat until the onion is soft and translucent. Adjust the heat so that the onions and garlic do not brown. Add the white wine and Pernod. Simmer for 5 minutes.

3. Add the FISH STOCK and tomatoes. Simmer for 15 minutes. Add 1 teaspoon of tomato paste if the soup needs more color. Add the scallops and salt and pepper to taste. Serve immediately, garnishing each bowl with ¼ teaspoon basil pesto stirred in just before serving.

FISH STOCK

1 medium onion, sliced
1 tablespoon butter
10 peppercorns
1 bouquet garni
1 cup dry white wine or the juice
  of ½ lemon (optional)

1½ pounds fish bones,
  broken into pieces
4-6 cups water
  Salt and white pepper to taste

In a kettle, sauté the onion in the butter until the onion is soft but not brown. Add all other ingredients and bring slowly to a boil, skimming the surface scum as necessary. As soon as the stock reaches a boil, reduce the heat and simmer, uncovered, for 20 minutes. Strain and season to taste.

Never boil fish stock or it will become bitter. Do not add fish skin to the stock as the skin will darken it.

FETTUCCINE WITH MORELS AND SWEETBREADS

1 *pound sweetbreads*
½ *pound fresh morels or*
    2 ounces dried morels
2 *medium onions, chopped*
2 *carrots, chopped*
1 *cup chopped celery*
⅛ *teaspoon thyme*
5 *cups WHITE VEAL STOCK*
1 *pound FETTUCCINE*
6 *shallots, minced*

4-5 *tablespoons clarified butter*
1 *cup vermouth plus*
    2 tablespoons for deglazing
3 *tablespoons white roux*
2 *cups heavy (whipping) cream*
    Salt and white pepper to taste
    Juice of ½ lemon
1 *bunch fresh tarragon, chopped*
    (approximately ½ ounce)

1. Rinse the sweetbreads in cold water for 2 to 3 hours, changing water frequently. If using dried morels, soak 4 to 5 hours.

2. In a medium saucepan, sauté the onions, carrots, celery, and thyme until the onions are translucent. Add the VEAL STOCK and sweetbreads. Add water if necessary to cover the sweetbreads. Simmer for 20 minutes. Cool the sweetbreads in the stock, making sure that the stock covers the sweetbreads. When cool, trim the skin from the sweetbreads, devein if necessary, and refrigerate in the stock overnight.

3. Boil the FETTUCCINE in salted water until *al dente*, 2 to 3 minutes for fresh pasta or 8 to 10 minutes for dried. Drain, cover with cold water, and reserve.

4. Remove the sweetbreads from the VEAL STOCK and set aside . Strain and reserve the VEAL STOCK.

5. In a medium saucepan, sauté 3 minced shallots in 2 tablespoons clarified butter until the shallots are translucent. Add the cup of vermouth and bring to a boil. Add the strained VEAL STOCK, thicken with 2 to 3 tablespoons of roux, and cook 15 to 20 minutes. Add 1 cup of cream and cook 10 minutes. Strain the vermouth cream sauce; add salt and pepper to taste. Reserve.

6. In a large pan, sauté the remaining shallots, the morels, and the sweet-breads in 2 tablespoons clarified butter. When the sweetbreads begin to brown, 4 to 6 minutes, deglaze with 2 tablespoons vermouth. When the vermouth has reduced to a thick syrup, add the lemon juice, 1 cup of cream, and the vermouth cream sauce. Reduce until the sauce thickens enough to just coat the back of a spoon. Adjust seasoning. Add the tarragon. Keep warm.

7. Submerge the FETTUCCINE in boiling water just long enough to heat through. Drain well. Toss with the morel and sweetbread sauce. Serve immediately.

Clarified butter is used to eliminate the milk solids that would mar the delicate cream sauce. To clarify butter, melt, remove any foam that rises to the surface, and spoon off the clear golden liquid.

Roux, the classic thickening agent used soups and sauces, is made by cooking equal amounts of butter and flour over low heat for 5 to 6 minutes. Roux must be stirred constantly while cooking. For a white roux, adjust the heat so that the roux does not brown. For a brown roux, allow the mixture to brown, but watch carefully so that it does not burn.

WHITE VEAL STOCK

4-5 *pounds veal bones, cracked*
    or cut into small pieces
  2 *onions, quartered*
  2 *carrots, quartered*
  2 *stalks celery, cut into*
    2-inch pieces

  1 *large bouquet garni*
10 *peppercorns*
  1 *head garlic, split with*
    skins left on
3-4 *quarts water*

1. Blanch the veal bones by bringing to a boil in water to cover; reduce heat and simmer 5 minutes. Drain. Rinse in cold water.

2. In a stock pot bring the veal bones, vegetables, bouquet garni, peppercorns, garlic, and the water slowly to a boil. Skim surface scum. Reduce the heat and simmer the stock 4 to 5 hours, skimming occasionally. The stock should reduce very slowly.

3. Strain the stock, discarding solids. If the flavor is not concentrated enough, boil again until reduced further. Chill quickly by placing the container of stock in running cold water. Skim off any fat before using. Stock can be kept 2 to 3 days in the refrigerator. Stock freezes well.

White veal stock is used for light sauces to serve with veal or poultry. This recipe makes 2 to 3 quarts of stock.

The classic bouquet garni is made of 1 sprig fresh or dried thyme, 1 bay leaf, and 10 to 12 parsley stems. Herbs can be either tied together with a string or placed in a piece of cheesecloth secured by string.

FETTUCCINE

5 *eggs, room temperature*   *Pinch of salt*
4 *cups all-purpose flour*

1. Mix the eggs, flour, and salt in a bowl or on a pastry board. Knead until the dough becomes smooth and elastic, 8 to 10 minutes. Cover with plastic wrap and let rest for 30 minutes.
2. Roll the dough to desired thickness and cut into ¼-inch strips. If using a pasta machine, knead and cut according to manufacturer's instructions.

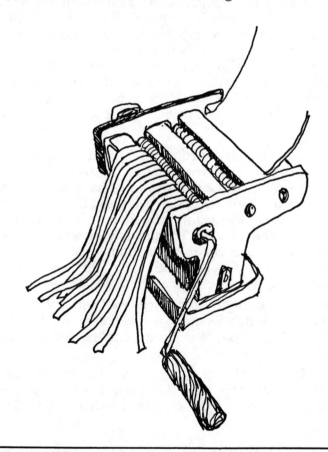

ROAST SQUAB WITH PORT WINE SAUCE AND WILD RICE

6 *whole squab*	*Salt and pepper to taste*
7 *shallots, chopped*	12 *cloves garlic, unpeeled*
4 *cloves garlic, chopped*	3 *ounces wild rice*
⅛ *teaspoon thyme*	3 *medium mushrooms, cleaned,*
1 *cup ruby port wine*	*stemmed, and sliced*
6 *cups BROWN VEAL STOCK*	6 *cloves unpeeled garlic,*
1 *tablespoon tomato paste*	*roasted in hot oven,*
2 *tablespoons brown roux*	*5 to 7 minutes*
(see index)	

1. To prepare the sauce, trim the squabs of necks and wings at the middle joint. Brown the trimmings with 6 chopped shallots, the chopped garlic, and the thyme in a saucepan over medium heat until the mixture is very dark and almost completely dry. Deglaze the saucepan with the port and reduce by slightly more than half. Add the BROWN VEAL STOCK and tomato paste. Simmer until reduced by ⅓, about 1 hour. Add approximately 2 tablespoons of brown roux to thicken. Bring to a simmer and cook for 10 minutes. Pass the sauce through a fine strainer. Add salt and pepper to taste.

2. To roast the squabs, salt and pepper each cavity and stuff with 2 unpeeled cloves of garlic. Truss the squabs with string to retain shape while roasting. Cook, breast side down, in a heavy skillet over high heat until lightly brown. Turn squabs on backs and finish in a hot (450°) oven for about 15 minutes for medium rare. Remove from the oven. Let set for 10 minutes before carving. Squabs may be served whole, but carving makes a more attractive presentation. Just before serving, remove the thighs and legs at the thigh-body joint, and remove the breast in two halves as close to the breast bone as possible.

3. To prepare the wild rice, rinse the rice very well with cold water. Boil the rice for 25 to 30 minutes. Drain off any excess water. Sauté with 1 chopped shallot and the sliced mushrooms until tender. Add salt and pepper to taste.

4. Spoon a layer of Port Wine Sauce on each serving plate. Place a mound of wild rice in the middle of the plate. Arrange the boned squab around the rice. Garnish each serving by placing a roasted clove of garlic on top of the rice.

A critical step in the recipe is the browning of the squab trimmings with the shallots, garlic, and thyme. Cooks will be tempted to stop the browning too soon. Care must be taken not to burn the mixture, but it must be cooked until it is very dark and almost completely dry in order to bring the proper color and flavor to the sauce. "Brown but not black" is the guide.

BROWN VEAL STOCK is used for brown sauces and for rich ragouts and braised dishes. Except for the addition of 1 tablespoon of tomato paste and half an onion singed over an electric plate or gas burner, the ingredients for BROWN VEAL STOCK are identical to those for WHITE VEAL STOCK (see index). The procedure is also the same for making the two stocks except for two crucial differences. Instead of blanching the bones as for white stock, for brown stock place the bones in a roasting pan and roast in a very hot oven (450°) for 30 to 40 minutes or until the bones are browned, stirring occasionally. Add the onions, carrots, and celery and brown. Transfer the browned bones and vegetables with a slotted spoon to a stockpot and proceed as for white veal stock except add the tomato paste and the singed half onion to the stock before simmering.

FLOATING ISLANDS WITH ORANGE SAUCE

ORANGE CUSTARD SAUCE

2 cups milk	5 tablespoons sugar
1 vanilla bean, split lengthwise	1 cup orange juice
4 egg yolks	Zest of 1 orange, chopped

1. Scald the milk with the vanilla bean in a saucepan. Remove from heat and let infuse for 10 minutes. Remove the vanilla bean, rinse, dry, and reserve for future use. Whisk the yolks and sugar together in a bowl until light and thick. Whisk in 1 cup of the milk until the mixture is smooth. Whisk the egg-milk mixture into the remaining 1 cup of milk in the saucepan. Cook over medium heat, stirring constantly, until thick enough to coat the back of a spoon, about 5 minutes. Do not boil or the eggs will curdle. Strain the custard through a fine strainer to remove any particles of vanilla bean or cooked egg. Strain and cool.

2. In a small saucepan, reduce the orange juice by ⅔ over medium heat. Add the orange zest. Remove from the heat, let cool, and stir into the custard sauce. Refrigerate until needed.

MERINGUE ISLANDS

4 egg whites	⅔ cup sugar

1. In an electric mixer or with a wire whisk, beat the egg whites until they stiffen and reach the "hard peak" stage. Add 2 tablespoons of sugar and whisk 1 more minute. Fold in the remaining sugar gradually; do not beat or the meringue will deflate.

2. Using a large serving spoon, form the meringue into individual quenelle-shaped ovals. Drop meringues into a pan containing at least 3 inches of barely simmering water or milk. Poach 30 seconds, turning once. Drain on towels and chill. Meringue Islands can be refrigerated for several hours.

CARAMEL

⅓ cup sugar   2 tablespoons water

1. In a small saucepan combine sugar and water. Boil over high heat until the sugar is dissolved and the syrup reaches light brown in color. Syrup will darken quickly and burn at the end of the caramelization process if not watched closely.

2. While the caramel syrup is still warm, drizzle over the Meringue Islands.

3. To serve: place 2 Meringue Islands for each person on a pool of the Orange Custand Sauce. Garnish each plate with 3 orange segments, membranes removed, if desired.

CASA GRANDE
·RESTAURANT·

Dinner for Six

Entremes de Ostiones Ahumados, Virginia

Potaje de Lentejas

Aguacates Rellenos con Camarones en Escabeche

Arroz con Pollo

Flan a la Antigua

Wines:

With the Appetizer and Salad—J. Lohr Chenin Blanc, 1983

With the Entrée—Torres Sangria de Torro

Maria and Ramon Cardenas and Family, Owners-Chefs

Maria and Ramon Cardenas have a mission: to educate the patrons of Casa Grande concerning the vast difference between the authentic food of their homeland and the various American versions of Mexican food. "Contrary to popular belief," Maria asserts, "Mexican food is not necessarily hot. It is festive, colorful, healthful food seasoned delicately or boldly at the discretion of the chef." And although she is pleased that customers applaud her enchiladas, chile rellenos, and flautas, Maria wishes more people would order such traditional, sophisticated specialities as Pollo Pibil (chicken steamed in banana leaves), Huachinago a la Veracruzana (red snapper Veracruz style), or one of the classic Spanish dishes that have become part of Mexican cuisine. An ambassador for Mexican cooking as well as a culinary artist, Maria encourages customers to place orders in advance for their favorite Mexican dish.

As suggested by the restaurant's logo—the Feathered Serpent, symbol of Quetzalcoatl, king-god of Toltec tradition—the Cardenas family is conscious and proud of its culinary heritage. "Mexican food is a blend of Indian, Spanish, French, and even Austrian and Italian cuisines. Over the centuries Mexicans have assimilated the best of these styles of cooking and have produced a cuisine that is truly cosmopolitan yet as distinctive as any in the world.

"I learned to cook as a child in Chihuahua, Mexico, from my mother, who was a wonderful cook," recalls Maria. She then studied with the famous Juarez chef, Virginia Prats, before moving first to New Mexico and then to San Francisco where she and Ramon opened the Jacaranda restaurant. They moved to Salt Lake City and opened Casa Grande in 1965 at the suggestion of Ramon's relatives. "They said there would be great opportunities for us here. They were right."

Casa Grande is a family enterprise, with Ramon, Jr., joining his parents in the kitchen. Daughter Lucy, also a good cook, manages the dining room. They recently opened a second restaurant, named Villa Señor in honor of Ramon, in the Admiral Byrd Plaza located in the Salt Lake City International Center adjacent to the airport. "Running two restaurants is easy," laughs Maria, "because everyone in the Cardenas family cooks." The result is Mexican cuisine at its finest.

177 East 200 South   533-0196
Salt Lake City

ENTREMES DE OSTIONES AHUMADOS, VIRGINIA

2 *large tomatoes, chopped*
2 *fresh Serrano or jalapeño*
   chiles, finely chopped
1 *small white onion, chopped*
2 *scallions, green part only,*
   chopped
2 *large, ripe avocados, peeled,*
   pitted, and halved
3 *tablespoons fresh cilantro,*
   chopped

1 *tablespoon lime juice*
   Salt
   Garlic powder
2-3 *cans smoked oysters, drained*
2 *cups shredded Monterey jack*
   cheese
   Lettuce leaves
   Tomato slices
   Warm tortillas

1. In a large glass or ceramic bowl, combine the tomatoes, chiles, onion, scallions, avocados, cilantro, and lime juice. While stirring gently to toss ingredients, cut the avocados into bite-size pieces. By this process the avocado will become soft and coat the other ingredients. Add salt, about 1½ teaspoons, and garlic powder, about ½ teaspoon, to taste. Cover and refrigerate until chilled.

2. Transfer the avocado mixture to an attractive serving platter. Top with smoked oysters and sprinkle with the cheese. Garnish with lettuce leaves and tomato slices.

3. Serve with a stack of warm, soft flour or corn tortillas. Traditionally, this appetizer is spooned into tortillas and eaten like taquitos.

The lime juice is an essential ingredient as it adds flavor and keeps the avocado from turning black. Garlic powder is used in this recipe because it allows more careful control of seasoning and because some people object to the somewhat bitter taste of uncooked garlic pieces.

The inspiration for this dish comes from my dear friend and tutor, Virginia Prats, the most famous chef in Juarez. It is named in honor of her.

POTAJE DE LENTEJAS

2 cups dried lentils
6½ cups water
2 teaspoons salt
1 small onion,
   peeled and halved
2 cloves garlic, peeled
3 strips bacon, cut in
   small pieces
½ small onion, chopped

½ medium green bell pepper,
   cut in thin slices
1 teaspoon finely chopped garlic
1 (6-ounce) can tomato paste
2 tablespoons fresh chopped
   cilantro
1 banana, sliced

1. Wash the lentils thoroughly. Add to a pot with 6 cups water, salt, onion, and garlic. Bring to a boil, lower heat, and simmer, covered, for about 45 minutes or until the lentils are just tender. Remove the onion and garlic; discard.

2. Make a sofrito by sautéing the bacon pieces in a skillet until they become brown but not crisp. Add the chopped onion, bell pepper, and chopped garlic. Cook until the vegetables are soft. Add the tomato paste and stir to combine.

3. Add the sofrito to the lentils. Rinse out the skillet in which the sofrito was cooked with ½ cup water and add to the lentils. Cook for 20 minutes, stirring frequently. Add salt to taste, if desired. If the soup seems too thick, add more water. Just before serving, stir in the cilantro.

4. Serve hot in individual bowls with sliced banana.

Some cooks remove the bacon from the sofrito before adding it to the lentils. The addition of banana slices to the soup is a regional preference that varies throughout Mexico. We think the bananas add a very special taste and texture to the soup.

AGUACATES RELLENOS CON CAMARONES EN ESCABECHE

1 pound fresh medium shrimp
¼ medium onion
1 lime, halved
Salt
½ cup olive oil
½ cup lime juice
1 tablespoon dry white wine
2 cloves garlic, mashed
1 small onion, thinly sliced
2 fresh or canned jalapeño chiles,
    cut into thin strips

1 tomato, chopped
8-10 green olives stuffed with
    pimento, chopped
Fresh ground black pepper
Sugar (optional)
2 teaspoons chopped cilantro
3-4 large avocados
MAYONESA DE AJO
Finely chopped cilantro
    for garnish
Lettuce leaves

1. Peel and devein the shrimp. In enough water to cover by 1-inch, boil the shrimp, ¼ onion, lime halves, and a pinch of salt until the shrimp just turn white and are just tender, about 2 minutes. Drain. Discard the onion and lime. Cut the shrimp in half, crosswise, and set aside.

2. In a large glass or ceramic bowl, combine the olive oil, lime juice, and wine. Add the garlic, onion slices, jalapeños, tomato, and olives. Add salt and pepper to taste, about 2 teaspoons each. If the marinade seems too sour, add approximately ¼ teaspoon sugar. Add the chopped cilantro and the cooked shrimp. Stir gently to combine. Refrigerate until chilled.

3. Just before serving, peel the avocados, slice in half lengthwise, and remove the pits. Dip into the shrimp marinade, covering all exposed surfaces, to prevent discoloration.

4. To serve, spoon the marinated shrimp and vegetable mixture into the avocado halves. Top with MAYONESA DE AJO. Sprinkle with cilantro. Serve on a bed of lettuce leaves.

MAYONESA DE AJO

2 egg yolks
3 cloves garlic, mashed
   to a paste

½ cup olive oil
2 teaspoons lime juice
2 teaspoons white wine
   Pinch of salt

In a blender or with a wire whisk, thoroughly blend the egg yolks and garlic. Add the oil, 1 tablespoon at a time, beating continuously until smooth, thick, and creamy. Add the lime juice and wine. Add salt to taste.

ARROZ CON POLLO

1 large chicken, about 3 pounds,
   cut into 6-8 serving pieces
   Salt
   Fresh ground black pepper
1 cup cooking oil
1 garlic clove, peeled
½ pound pork shoulder, cut into
   bite-size pieces
¼ pound smoked ham,
   cut into small chunks
1 cup finely chopped onion
1 medium green bell pepper,
   sliced into thin strips
1 tablespoon finely chopped
   garlic
2 cups long grain rice
   (Uncle Ben's converted)

1 (6-ounce) can tomato paste
1 teaspoon saffron threads,
   crushed (or saffron powder),
   soaked in ½ cup water
½ cup dry white wine
4 cups boiling water
1 cup fresh or frozen green peas
1 small can red pimento,
   in strips
½ cup green pitted olives
½ cup black pitted olives
6-8 medium raw shrimp, shelled,
   deveined, and cut in half
1 tablespoon finely chopped
   parsley

1. Rinse the chicken pieces and pat completely dry with paper toweling. Sprinkle with salt and freshly ground black pepper. Set aside.

2. In a large, flame-proof casserole dish or a large pot suitable for table service, heat the oil and garlic clove over moderate heat until the garlic begins to turn brown. Remove the garlic and discard.

3. Add to the hot oil the chicken, pork, and ham. Cook until browned evenly, about 10 minutes. Remove the chicken and set aside.

4. To the pork and ham, add the chopped onion, bell pepper, and garlic. Sauté until the onion is translucent and the pepper soft, about 5 minutes. Add the rice, stirring well to absorb liquids. Stir in the tomato paste. Add the saffron water, the white wine, and the boiling water. Add salt, about 2 teaspoons, and fresh ground black pepper, about 1 teaspoon, to taste. Return the chicken to the pot. Bring to a boil, then reduce heat to low. Stir in the peas, pimento, olives, shrimp, and parsley. Bring to a boil again. Immediately reduce the heat, cover, and simmer 20 to 30 minutes or until the chicken is tender and the rice has aborbed all the liquid.

5. Serve directly from the casserole or pot.

For perfect rice, use 2½ cups of liquid for each cup of rice. For a richer taste, use chicken stock or fortify water with chicken base or bouillon cubes.

Arroz con Pollo is a simplified version of paella. (The term "paella" refers to a kind of cooking utensil, not a recipe for a particular dish.) It is a classic Spanish dish that has become an important part of Mexican cuisine. We often offer Spanish dishes in recognition of our culinary heritage.

Add any available pork or ham bones to the pot in Step 3 of the recipe for greater flavor. Remove the bones before serving.

FLAN A LA ANTIGUA

2 cups sugar
4 cups milk
8 cloves

1 stick cinnamon
4 eggs
1 teaspoon vanilla
Strawberries for garnish

1. Heat a small saucepan over medium heat. Add 1 cup of sugar and let it melt without stirring to prevent crystallization. When the sugar is melted and translucent, increase the heat and stir constantly until it reaches a rich caramel color. Immediately pour the carmelized sugar into a 9-inch glass pie plate, quickly tipping and rotating to coat the bottom of the plate evenly. Set aside to cool.

2. In another saucepan, bring the milk, cloves, and cinnamon to a boil. Remove from the heat and let cool for 5 minutes.

3. Using an electric mixer, beat the eggs on high speed until well beaten and frothy, about 1 minute. Add the remaining cup of sugar and beat until well blended, about 1 more minute.

4. Strain the milk. Pour the milk into the egg mixture and beat vigorously to incorporate, about 30 seconds. Stir in the vanilla.

5. Pour the custard mixture into the caramel-coated pie plate. Place in a larger shallow container filled with enough water to reach half way up the side of the pie plate. Place the custard in the water bath in a pre-heated 350° oven. Bake for 45 to 55 minutes. The flan will appear to be soft, but will set as it cools. Let cool, then refrigerate until serving.

6. Just before serving, unmold the flan by inverting it onto a plate large enough to hold the small pool of caramel sauce. Garnish with whole, fresh strawberries.

There are many varieties of flan, most of them containing fruits—pineapple, coconut, even pumpkin. This caramel-coated, vanilla custard flan is the most traditional of all as the name suggests; we think it cannot be improved upon.

Dinner for Six

Carpaccio

Oysters Florentine

Leek and Shrimp Salad

Chicken Pignole

Cantaloupe Sorbet

Wines:

With the Carpaccio—Beaulieu Cabernet Sauvignon, 1978

With the Oysters—Laboure-Roi Montrachet, 1981

With the Salad—Acacia Chardonnay, 1982

With the Chicken—Antonin Rodet, Meursault, 1979

With the Sorbet—Heidsieck Champagne, 1979

Triad/La Caille Ventures

Chris Stathis, Executive Chef

U tah's "most elegant mansion in its heyday," the Devereaux House was the center of Salt Lake City social life during the territorial period. Now restored as a restaurant, Devereaux features lavish decorations and period furnishings as well as a special dining experience. Located in the center of the futuristic Triad Center, Devereaux brings the past to the present. Guests approach the restaurant along the circular drive just as horses and carriages did when the original owners, the William Jennings family, occupied the residence in the nineteenth century.

Each of the commodious rooms is decorated differently to accentuate the mood of the dining experience. For example, an upstairs Board Room sets the tone for business lunches and dinners while the downstairs Parlor, with its authentic Utah stone fireplace, is perfect for a women's luncheon or intimate dinner. Deborah Johnson, wife of co-owner David Johnson, carefully researched period decor before supervising the interior design. The result is a step into the gracious past of Utah's history.

Northern Italian cuisine is the emphasis of this recent addition to Salt Lake's dining scene. The kitchen is under the direction of Chef Chris Stathis, who started his culinary career at 15 and gained experience and expertise in West Coast restaurants. Stathis has quickly caught on to local dining habits, for his food is well prepared and the portions generous. With seating for over 200 guests, Devereaux House, a popular setting for wedding receptions and private parties, is once again a center of Salt Lake social life.

Devereaux Plaza   575-5200
III Triad Center
300 West and South Temple Streets

CARPACCIO

1 pound beef tenderloin
1 medium onion, thinly sliced
1 stalk celery, thinly sliced
2 cloves garlic
½ lemon, thinly sliced
2 cups dry red wine
2 cups red wine vinegar
1 cup brown sugar
12 parsley stems
½ orange, thinly sliced

½ cup capers
2 tablespoons pickling spice
2 tablespoons salt
Leaf lettuce
Finely chopped onion,
 for garnish
Capers, for garnish
Orange wedges or lemon slices,
 for garnish

1. Remove all fat and tendons from the tenderloin. Place in the freezer to firm, 15 to 20 minutes.

2. Combine the remaining ingredients in a non-aluminum pot. Bring to a boil, reduce heat, and simmer for 10 minutes. Cool and strain. Discard solids. Reserve marinade.

3. With a sharp knife or slicing machine, cut the tenderloin into paper thin slices. Arrange the tenderloin slices in a non-corrodible pan, cover with marinade, and refrigerate for 1 hour before serving.

4. To serve, arrange tenderloin slices on a bed of leaf lettuce. Place a small mound of finely chopped onions and capers in the center. Sprinkle with marinade. Garnish with orange wedges or sliced lemon, if desired.

OYSTERS FLORENTINE

MORNAY SAUCE
4 cups spinach leaves, washed, dried, and torn into bite-size pieces
Salt and white pepper to taste

36 oysters
4 ounces Parmesan cheese, grated
Leaf lettuce
Lemon wedges, for garnish

1. Prepare the MORNAY SAUCE. Fold in the spinach leaves. Add salt and white pepper to taste.

2. Clean and shuck the oysters. Pry the meat loose from the shell and replace it on a half-shell retaining as much of the juice as possible. Place the oysters on a baking sheet and place under a broiler for 30 seconds.

3. Remove from the broiler. Top each oyster with Mornay-Spinach Sauce and sprinkle with grated Parmesan cheese. Return to the broiler until the sauce is bubbling and the cheese is beginning to brown, about 45 seconds.

4. Serve oysters on a bed of leaf lettuce. Garnish with a lemon wedge.

MORNAY SAUCE

3 cups chicken broth
1 cup dry white wine
4 tablespoons flour
4 tablespoons butter

1 tablespoon lemon juice
½ cup grated Parmesan cheese
2 cups heavy (whipping) cream
Salt and white pepper to taste

1. Bring the chicken stock and wine to a boil over medium high heat. Reduce heat and simmer 5 minutes.

2. Meanwhile, combine the flour, butter, and lemon juice in another pan. Cook, stirring constantly, over medium low heat for 5 to 6 minutes. Take care not to let the roux brown.

3. Add the roux to the chicken stock and simmer until sufficiently thickened to coat lightly the back of a spoon. Add the cheese and cream. Reduce over medium heat until the sauce coats the back of a spoon. Add salt and pepper to taste.

LEEK AND SHRIMP SALAD

12 *medium leeks, white part only*
 1 *quart chicken stock,*
    canned or homemade
    VINAIGRETTE DRESSING
 6 *large lettuce leaves, washed,*
    dried, and crisped

12 *ounces small bay shrimp*
 1 *whole pimento, canned,*
    cut lengthwise into
    24 julienne strips

1. Clean the leeks and wash thoroughly. Place in a pot of boiling chicken stock to cover and simmer gently until tender, 45 to 60 minutes. Transfer leeks to an ice bath to cool. Save leek flavored chicken stock for another use.

2. Remove the leeks from the ice bath when cool. Place in a dish. Pour about ½ of the VINAIGRETTE DRESSING over the leeks and refrigerate 24 to 48 hours before serving.

3. To serve, arrange 2 leeks per person on a lettuce leaf on a chilled plate. Mound the shrimp in the center and drape with 4 pimento slices. Combine VINAIGRETTE marinade with reserved dressing. Pour over entire salad.

VINAIGRETTE DRESSING

 1 *tablespoon minced pimento*
 1 *tablespoon minced onion*
 ½ *dill pickle, minced*
1½ *teaspoons capers*
 1 *teaspoon salt*

 ½ *teaspoon Dijon mustard*
 3 *teaspoons fresh lemon juice*
 6 *teaspoons red wine vinegar*
 1 *tablespoon minced parsley*
 1 *cup olive oil*

Combine all ingredients and blend well. Use about ½ of the VINAIGRETTE to marinate the leeks. Reserve the remaining VINAIGRETTE for dressing the salad.

CHICKEN PIGNOLE

6 *whole chicken breasts,*
  boned and trimmed,
  but not skinned

¼ *pound butter*
  PINE NUT STUFFING
  Olive oil

1. Liberally rub the inside of each whole chicken breast with 1 to 2 tablespoons butter. Place a mound of PINE NUT STUFFING in the center of the breast. Fold sides of the breast over the stuffing to cover. Seal breasts with toothpicks.

2. Place sealed breasts, seam side down, in a roasting pan lightly coated with olive oil. Rub olive oil over the exposed skin of each breast. Bake in a 375° oven for 25 to 30 minutes or until the skin is golden brown.

PINE NUT STUFFING

6 *eggs*
6 *ounces Parmesan cheese,*
  grated
12 *ounces feta cheese,*
  chopped into into ½-inch dice
2 *tablespoons finely minced basil*
6 *ounces shelled pine nuts*
½ *medium onion, minced*

2 *tablespoons commercial*
  poultry seasoning
1 *teaspoon salt*
1 *teaspoon white pepper*
1½ *cups milk*
6 *slices bread, toasted, crust*
  removed, and cut into
  1-inch squares

Combine all ingredients, mixing well to incorporate.

CANTALOUPE SORBET

1 tablespoon honey
3 tablespoons fresh lemon juice
1 cup sugar

1 cup water
2 large or 3 medium cantaloupes
3 tablespoons brandy

1. Bring honey, lemon juice, sugar, and water to a boil over medium heat. Cook for 5 minutes. Let cool.
2. Seed the cantaloupes. With a melon baller make 18 cantaloupe balls. Soak the melon balls in brandy. Set aside for garnish.
3. Cut the rest of the cantaloupe flesh into 1-inch pieces and purée in a food processor until there are 3 cups of purée.
4. Combine the cooled honey-sugar syrup and the cantaloupe purée. Mix well and freeze in an ice cream machine according to manufacturer's instructions. Transfer to a plastic container and store in the freezer until needed, no more than 3 days.
5. Allow the frozen sorbet to thaw slightly before serving to enhance the flavor. Serve with brandied cantaloupe balls as a garnish.

Honeydew melon may be substituted for cantaloupe; if so, substitute lime juice for the lemon juice. Sorbets can be made without a special ice cream maker. After mixing syrup and puree, pour the mixture into a shallow pan or two metal ice cube trays. Place in the freezer until almost frozen. Break the semifrozen sorbet into chunks and reprocess in a food processor until smooth. Repeat the refreezing and reprocessing a second or, preferably, a third time.

Glitretind
GOURMET ROOM

Dinner for Four

Danish Camembert en Croute

Seafood Stew

Shrimp Salad Marie

Roast Goose with Apple and Prune Stuffing

Norwegian Apple Tart

Wines:

With the Camembert—Joseph Phelps Gewürtztraminer, 1982

With the Stew—Gran Cru Sonoma Sauvignon Blanc, 1983

With the Goose—Chateauneuf-du-Pape, Lazaret, 1982

Paul Dougan and Rick Prince, Owners

Anthony De Hoop, Executive Chef

Nestled among the aspen and spruce mid-point on Bald Mountain in the Deer Valley ski resort complex is the Stein Eriksen Lodge, one of the nation's most beautiful and luxurious alpine lodges. The massive stone and timber lodge, at once traditional and contemporary, is named in honor of the legendary Norwegian Olympic gold medalist of 1952 who is the resort's director of skiing. From the underground parking and heated walkways to the elegant furnishings and snappy service, everything about the lodge exudes a touch of class with a European flair for finesse.

The huge kitchen, which produces sumptuous Sunday brunches winter and summer, services two restaurants—the Birkebeiner, for light, casual fare, and the Glitretind Gourmet Room, for elegant, formal dining. Although as varied as its clientele, the Glitretind menu has a decided Scandinavian flavor ranging from classic appetizers such as Gravlax and Rumaki to entrées such as Gaasteg med aebler og Suedker to dessert specialties. As indicated by the complimentary appetizer of fruit and cheese or pâté served on a silver tray with an artful arrangement of garnishes, the staff pays particular attention to the presentation of its food.

Lush green carpeting and coral-colored upholstered oak chairs in French Provincial style give the dining room an aura of delicate sophistication that contrasts effectively with the massive ruggedness of the mountain environment visible through the windows. Summer or winter, the 40-mile drive from Salt Lake City to the Stein Eriksen Lodge brings memorable culinary as well as scenic rewards, for the Glitretind, living up to its name, is gastronomically "a shining mountain."

Stein Eriksen Lodge   649-3700
Deer Valley

DANISH CAMEMBERT EN CROUTE

4 *(4-inch square) pieces*
  puff pastry dough
  Egg wash
4 *(4½-ounce) tins Danish*
  Camembert (Tiny Dane)

  Butter
8 *strawberries, sliced*
1 *apple, sliced*
4 *small bunches grapes*
½ *cup toasted almond slices*

1. Brush the egg wash over a piece of the puff pastry dough. Place 1 whole 4½-ounce round of the Danish Camembert in the center of the dough. Fold the dough over the top of the cheese, pressing to seal seams. Place the Camembert en Croute, seam side down, on a buttered baking sheet. Repeat with the other 3 pieces of dough and cheese.

2. Preheat the oven to 350°. Brush the exposed dough with the egg wash. Bake until the dough is puffed and golden brown, about 20 minutes.

3. Serve each person 1 whole Camembert en Croute garnished with 2 sliced strawberries, 3 to 4 apple slices, and 1 small bunch of grapes. Top with almond slices.

Danish Camembert differs noticeably in taste and texture from its Swiss and French counterparts. Cheese en croute can also be used for a buffet dinner or cocktail party. Simply use a larger piece of cheese and a larger square of puff pastry dough.

SEAFOOD STEW

2 tablespoons butter
2 leeks, white part only, diced
3 celery stalks, diced
2 tablespoons flour
1 cup fish stock (see index)
4 cups heavy (whipping) cream
    or half and half

1½ pounds seafood combination
     (salmon, crab, scallops)
     in bite-size pieces
¼-½ cup dry sherry to taste
1 teaspoon thyme
2-3 dashes Tabasco sauce to taste
     Salt and white pepper to taste
     Butter
1 tablespoon chopped parsley

1. Melt the butter in a medium pot. Sauté the leeks and celery until crisp-tender, 5 to 7 minutes. Sprinkle in the flour, stirring well to incorporate, and cook 2 to 3 minutes. Slowly add the fish stock, stirring to blend well. Add the cream and bring to a boil. Immediately reduce the heat and simmer for 10 minutes. Add the seafood and cook 5 minutes. Stir in the sherry. Add the thyme. Season with the Tabasco, salt, and white pepper to taste.

2. Serve hot in individual bowls. Garnish with ½ pat of butter and a sprinkling of chopped parsley. Pass around additional sherry as desired.

Any combination of shellfish and firm white fish works well—shrimp, lobster, swordfish, red snapper, or cod are good choices. Salmon is especially good to use because it adds color as well as flavor to the stew. Because each fish has a different taste, the final seasoning will vary according to the kind of seafood used.

The small quantity of fish or seafood stock needed for the stew can be made by simmering bones and shells of the seafood to be used. Any bones or shells can also be simmered in commercial clam juice for a more flavorful stock. Lobster or clam base will also work.

SHRIMP SALAD MARIE

1 cucumber, peeled, seeded, quartered, sliced on the bias
15 snow peas, strings removed
2 carrots, cut into thin julienne strips
1 small zucchini, sliced

1 small yellow squash, sliced
2 stalks celery, cut on the bias
1 green onion, chopped
½ pound medium shrimp, shelled, deveined, halved lengthwise
TARRAGON VINAIGRETTE

Combine the vegetables and shrimp in a large bowl. Toss gently with the TARRAGON VINAIGRETTE.

TARRAGON VINAIGRETTE

½ teaspoon Dijon mustard   ¼ teaspoon oregano
1 egg yolk   1 teaspoon sugar
3 tablespoons tarragon vinegar   ½ cup olive oil
1 teaspoon tarragon   Pinch garlic powder
¼ teaspoon marjoram   Salt and white pepper

With a wire whisk, blend together the mustard, egg yolk, tarragon vinegar, tarragon, marjoram, oregano, and sugar. Slowly add the olive oil, whisking constantly, until the dressing reaches a smooth, creamy consistency. Add the garlic powder, salt, and white pepper to taste. Adjust the seasonings.

The vinaigrette dressing should be made a day ahead in order to allow flavors to develop. The egg yolk serves as an emulsion which will prevent the dressing from separating. In fact, the entire salad is much improved in flavor if made up a day ahead and stored covered in the refrigerator. Toss again just prior to serving.

ROAST GOOSE WITH APPLE AND PRUNE STUFFING

1 (10-12 pound) whole goose
1 tablespoon thyme
1 tablespoon rosemary
1 tablespoon sage

Salt
Fresh ground black pepper
APPLE AND PRUNE STUFFING
BRANDIED CURRANT
  ORANGE SAUCE

1. Rinse and dry the goose. Reserve the neck, gizzard, and heart for making stock for the BRANDIED CURRANT ORANGE SAUCE. Rub the seasonings into the skin of the goose. Cover with plastic wrap and refrigerate overnight.

2. Bring the goose to room temperature before roasting. Fill the cavity of the goose with the APPLE AND PRUNE STUFFING. Truss the goose with heavy string. Place the goose on a poultry rack in a large roasting pan. Lightly pierce the skin all over, especially around the breast and thighs, to draw off fat while roasting. Roast in a preheated 450° oven for 15 minutes. Reduce the temperature to 375° and continue roasting, occasionally basting the goose with accumulated drippings, about 20 minutes per pound or until the juices run clear when the thigh is pricked with a fork.

3. Let the goose rest 15 to 20 minutes before carving. Serve with the APPLE AND PRUNE STUFFING. Pass the BRANDIED CURRANT ORANGE SAUCE.

APPLE AND PRUNE STUFFING can be baked separately. While the roast goose is resting before carving, spoon the stuffing into a greased pan, cover with foil, and bake in a 350° oven for 15 to 20 minutes.

Only the goose breast is served at the restaurant. To do the same at home, cut the breast in two pieces, skin left on, from the whole goose. Sprinkle with salt, fresh ground black pepper, and 1 teaspoon each thyme, rosemary, and sage. Wrap in plastic wrap and refrigerate overnight. Roast, skin side down, in a 425° oven for 20 minutes on the top oven shelf. Divide each breast half into two equal parts. Cut into thin slices. Top with BRANDIED CURRANT ORANGE SAUCE and accompany with APPLE AND PRUNE STUFFING. The thighs and legs of the goose can be used for another purpose (pâtés or salads) or seasoned and roasted with the breasts. If only roasting part of the goose, use the carcass bones for stock.

APPLE AND PRUNE STUFFING

1 (16-ounce) loaf French-style
  bread, cut into ½-inch cubes

3 apples, peeled, cored, and
  cut into ½-inch dice

1 (16-ounce) can pitted prunes,
  drained

¼ cup prune juice (from the
  canned prunes)

4 eggs

6 ounces apple juice
  Sage to taste
  Salt and pepper to taste

Thoroughly combine all ingredients. If the stuffing seems too dry, add more prune or apple juice. Roast the stuffing in the goose cavity or bake separately.

If there is any stuffing left from filling the goose cavity, it can be baked separately and served as additional portions or frozen for future use.

BRANDIED CURRANT AND ORANGE SAUCE

Goose neck, gizzard, and heart
1 small onion, peeled
1 stalk celery, coarsely chopped
1 carrot, coarsely chopped
6 cups water (approximately)
¼ cup currants
¼ cup brandy
3 tablespoons flour

3 tablespoons goose fat
Juice of ½ orange
Zest of ½ orange, grated
2 ounces Grand Marnier
2-3 teaspoons brown sugar
Pinch thyme
Pinch sage
Salt and pepper to taste

1. Make a goose stock by combining the goose neck, gizzard, heart, onion, celery, and carrot in water to cover, about 6 cups. Bring to a boil. Reduce the heat, skim off any surface scum, and simmer 2 to 3 hours, or until the stock is reduced by half. Strain the stock and remove any surface grease.

2. While the stock is cooking, marinate the currants in the brandy for at least 30 minutes.

3. Make a roux by mixing the flour with an equal amount of goose fat from the stock or from the roasting goose. Cook 10 to 12 minutes, stirring frequently. Adjust the heat to avoid excessive browning.

4. Stir the roux, 1 tablespoon at a time, into the goose stock to thicken to the consistency of a light gravy. Bring the stock to a boil, reduce the heat, and simmer 5 to 8 minutes. Strain.

5. Add the currants, brandy marinade, orange juice, orange zest, Grand Marnier, and brown sugar. Season to taste with the thyme, sage, salt, and pepper. Simmer gently for 20 minutes. If the stock becomes too thick, thin with additional orange juice. Adjust seasonings.

6. Serve as an accompaniment to the roast goose.

NORWEGIAN APPLE TART

CRUST:

½ teaspoon salt
2 tablespoons sugar
1½ cups flour

¼ pound butter
2 tablespoons sour cream
2 tablespoons almond paste
1 tablespoon vinegar

1. In a large mixing bowl, combine the salt, sugar, and flour. Cut the butter into small pieces and cut into the dry ingredients with a pastry blender, fork, or fingers until the mixture resembles a coarse meal.

2. In a small bowl, thoroughly blend the sour cream, almond paste, and vinegar. Add to the butter-flour mixture and work with fingers or a wooden spoon until the dough forms a rough mass. If the dough is too dry (crumbly), add water to moisten. Shape the dough into a ball and refrigerate, covered with plastic wrap, for at least 1 hour.

3. On a lightly floured work surface, roll out the dough to a circle ⅛-inch thick. Place the dough in a 10-inch tart tin, pressing to cover all corners or indentations. Place a piece of aluminum foil over the surface of the dough and fill with dried beans. Bake in a preheated 350° oven for 15 minutes. Remove the beans and aluminum foil. Return the tart shell to the oven and bake another 5 minutes to dry the center of the shell. Set aside.

FILLING:

4-6 green apples, peeled, cored, and cut into ½-inch cubes
½ teaspoon almond extract
½ teaspoon cinnamon
¼ teaspoon allspice
⅛ teaspoon ground cloves

½ cup brown sugar
1 teaspoon grated lemon zest
2 tablespoons lemon juice
2 tablespoons cornstarch
1 tablespoon apple juice
¼ cup currants
½ cup grated Gjetost cheese

In a large bowl, combine the apples, almond extract, spices, brown sugar, lemon zest, and lemon juice. Mix well. Sprinkle with the cornstarch, apple juice, currants, and cheese. Mix well.

Gjetost, a chocolate colored, nutty-flavored, Norwegian cheese made from goat milk is available in any good cheese shop.

TOPPING:

1½	cups flour	¼	teaspoon salt
½	teaspoon cinnamon	½	cup brown sugar
¼	teaspoon allspice	¼	cup butter
⅛	teaspoon ground cloves	2	tablespoons almond paste
1	teaspoon grated lemon zest	½	cup grated Gjetost cheese

Thoroughly combine the flour, spices, lemon zest, salt, and brown sugar. Cut the butter and almond paste into small pieces and cut, with a pastry blender or fingers, into the dry ingredients. The mixture should be crumbly. Stir in the grated cheese.

To Bake:

Fill the prebaked tart Crust with the apple Filling. Cover with Topping. Place the tart tin on a baking sheet and bake in a preheated 375° oven for 30 minutes. Serve warm for optimum flavor.

THE **Golden Cliff**

Dinner for Six

Chicken Liver Pâté with Fresh Pear Chutney

Mixed Wild Greens and Wild Flower Salad
with Bacon Parmesan Vinaigrette

Shrimp and Pasta al Pesto

Sour Cream Cashew Bread

Peach Raspberry Pie

Golden Cliff Cheesecake

Deep Powder Punch

Wines:

With the Pâté—a slightly chilled Beaujolais-Villages, 1982

With the Shrimp and Pasta—Far Niente Chardonnay, 1982

With the Pie—Chateau St. Jean Late Harvest Gewürztraminer, 1978

With the Cheesecake—Quady Vintage Port, 1978

Neil A. Cohen, Director of Club Operations

Robert L. Sullivan Jr., Chef

Nestled among the towering peaks of the Wasatch Mountains in Little Cottonwood Canyon, The Club at Snowbird, part of the Snowbird Ski and Summer Resort complex, offers a variety of outstanding dining experiences. Located in the Cliff Lodge, the private club, open to the public for a nominal guest membership fee, encompasses four distinct dining facilities: The Eagle's Nest Lounge for cocktails and a raw seafood bar, The Lodge Club for light lunches and dinners, The Mexican Keyhole for traditional south-of-the-border fare, and The Golden Cliff Restaurant for sumptuous international cuisine as well as special buffets and Sunday brunches. The operation of The Club is under the supervision of Cornell Hotel School Graduate Neil Cohen, a wine connoisseur who has compiled excellent wine lists to accompany the food served in each facility.

The Golden Cliff serves fine food amid the tastefully informal decor of a mountain resort. Two-story, wall-wide picture windows offer diners a magnificent view of the mountains that changes seasonally. Chef Robert Sullivan, who majored in philosophy as an undergraduate at the University of Vermont, emphasizes the creative and aesthetic dimensions of food preparation. "Cooking is an artistic event in the kitchen. It is an exciting opportunity to experiment with subtle flavorings and food combinations with the goal of pleasing people."

The Golden Cliff emphasizes fresh seafood, featuring specials as diverse as Jamaican snapper and Mako shark. "People are really surprised by the variety of fresh seafood we serve in the middle of the mountains, even in midwinter. It's a challenge to arrange for seafood to be flown in three times a week from the East and West coasts, but it's definitely worth the effort."

The Cliff Lodge   521-6040
Snowbird Ski and Summer Resort
Snowbird

CHICKEN LIVER PÂTÉ with FRESH PEAR CHUTNEY

6 medium mushrooms,
  cleaned but not stemmed
½ cup plus 1 tablespoon Madeira
2 tablespoons clarified butter
4 tablespoons pork fat, chopped
  (fresh or from mildly
  cured ham)
2 pounds chicken livers, rinsed
2 tablespoons heavy (whipping)
  cream
1½ teaspoons dry vermouth
⅛ teaspoon salt
⅛ teaspoon pepper

⅛ teaspoon dried basil
⅛ teaspoon dried sage
⅛ teaspoon celery salt
⅛ teaspoon minced garlic
1 tablespoon tomato paste
  Olive oil
6 lettuce leaves
  FRESH PEAR CHUTNEY
2 hardboiled eggs, chopped
½ Bermuda (red) onion,
  thinly sliced
  Capers
  Unsalted crackers

1. Poach the mushrooms in ½ cup Madeira until tender, 5 to 6 minutes. Drain. Reserve the mushrooms and the cooking liquid.

2. Melt the butter in a large skillet over medium high heat. Add the pork fat and render 6 to 7 minutes, taking care not to brown the pork pieces too heavily. Remove pork with a slotted spoon. Reserve.

3. Reduce heat to medium, add the chicken livers and 1½ tablespoons of the reserved Madeira cooking liquid. Sauté the livers until cooked to a light brownish pink inside, about 5 minutes on each side.

4. Transfer the livers with cooking liquid to a blender or food processor. Add the cream, 1 tablespoon of Madeira, the vermouth, spices, tomato paste, and 1 teaspoon of the reserved Madeira cooking liquid. Blend until very smooth, at least 5 minutes. Adjust seasonings.

5. Lightly coat bottom and sides of a 2x8x2-inch pâté mold with olive oil. Pour ⅓ of the pâté into the mold. Wet back of fingers in warm water and tamp the pâté fimly to remove air bubbles or holes. Press the reserved mushrooms, stem side down, in a row down the middle of the pâté. Add ⅓ of the pâté and tamp down as before. Add the final ⅓ of the pâté and tamp again. Cover and refrigerate for at least 8 hours.

continued...

6. For each serving, place two or three ¼-inch slices of pâté on a lettuce leaf accompanied by FRESH PEAR CHUTNEY. Garnish with chopped egg, thin slices of Bermuda onion, capers, and an unsalted cracker.

For a distinctly different taste, lay bacon strips across the width of the pâté mold. Fill with pâté as directed. Fold bacon strips across the top. Place the mold in a pan with enough water to come ¾ up the side of the mold. Bake in a 325° oven for 1 hour. Serve at room temperature or chilled.

FRESH PEAR CHUTNEY

2½ cups coarsely chopped pears
    (approximately 2 large pears
    peeled and cored)
½ cup finely chopped
    Granny Smith apples
¾ cup cider vinegar
1¼ cups seedless raisins
1½ tablespoons finely chopped
    green onion, white part only
 1 tablespoon chopped
    yellow onion

2 tablespoons grated fresh
   ginger (do not substitute
   dry ginger)
2 teaspoons ground allspice
¾ teaspoon ground cloves
1 teaspoon salt
½ teaspoon lemon juice
1½ cups granulated sugar
⅓ cup brown sugar

Place all of the ingredients except the two sugars in a saucepan and heat until bubbling. Immediately add the granulated and brown sugar. Stir well and let cook at a rolling boil for 10 to 15 minutes. Skim foam if necessary. Let cool and refrigerate until needed. Makes about 4 cups.

For a variation, substitute green tomatoes or other fruits for the pears or reverse the proportion of apples to pears. Canned fruit can be used.

MIXED WILD GREENS AND WILD FLOWER SALAD

½ *head escarole*
2 *cups beet greens*
⅓ *cup watercress*
⅓ *cup cilantro*
2⅓ *cups leaf lettuce, spinach,*
endive, mustard greens, or
any combination of greens

½ *cup dandelion leaves*
A variety of edible flower petals,
violets, marigolds, columbine,
nasturtiums, zucchini
blossoms, pumpkin blossoms
BACON PARMESAN
VINAIGRETTE

1. Wash and dry the greens. Tear into pieces (the cilantro should be in very small pieces) and chill.

2. Just before serving, combine the greens and flower petals in a large bowl. Toss with VINAIGRETTE. Top each serving with a whole columbine flower, pistils and stamens removed. If not using flowers, garnish greens with croutons and an anchovy.

BACON PARMESAN VINAIGRETTE

5 *shallots, finely minced*
4 *cloves garlic, finely minced*
½ *cup grated Parmesan cheese*
½ *cup grated Romano cheese*
6 *strips bacon, cooked crisp*
and finely chopped
⅓ *teaspoon oregano*
⅓ *teaspoon basil*
⅛ *teaspoon sage*
¼ *teaspoon thyme*
¼ *teaspoon cayenne pepper*

½ *teaspoon black pepper,*
coarsely ground
1 *tablespoon Worcestershire sauce*
1½ *tablespoons soy sauce*
½ *cup red wine vinegar*
½ *cup cider vinegar*
1 *tablespoon lemon juice*
1½ *tablespoons finely minced*
fresh parsley
3 *cups olive oil*

Combine all ingredients, mix well, and chill for at least 2 hours. Recombine before serving.

For an attractive appearance, salad greens should be torn in pieces of different sizes. A tossed green salad should always be served on a chilled plate. A good rule is to serve chilled food on chilled plates, warm food on warm plates.

SHRIMP AND PASTA AL PESTO

3 tablespoons olive oil	PESTO
1½ pounds SPINACH FETTUCCINE	6 lemon wedges
24 large shrimp, peeled and deveined	6 cherry tomatoes
2 tablespoons white wine	1 cup grated Parmesan and Romano cheese, mixed
Juice of ¼ lemon	

1. In a large pot, bring 1 gallon of water and 1 tablespoon of olive oil to a boil. Add the pasta and cook at a boil, stirring occasionally, for 10 to 12 minutes or until pasta is *al dente*. Drain.

2. While the pasta is cooking, heat 2 tablespoons of olive oil in a large skillet. Add the shrimp, white wine, and lemon juice. Sauté over medium heat until the shrimp are just pink and semi-translucent, about 1½ minutes on each side.

3. Add the FETTUCCINE to the skillet and toss with the shrimp. Add ⅔ of the pesto and a splash of lemon juice. Toss for 30 seconds. Add more pesto if desired.

4. To serve, fill the center of a warm plate with the FETTUCCINE. Arrange 4 shrimp on each plate. Garnish with a lemon wedge and a cherry tomato. Sprinkle with grated cheese.

Coordinate cooking the pasta and shrimp carefully so that neither suffers from overcooking. It is easier to hold the pasta than the shrimp. If necessary, drain the cooked pasta, reserve, and plunge into boiling water to warm when needed.

SPINACH FETTUCCINE

8 eggs, room temperature	1 clove garlic, finely minced
1 bunch spinach, leaves washed and dried	1 teaspoon salt
	6 cups all-purpose flour or semolina (approximately)

1. In an electric mixer or food processor, blend the eggs, spinach, garlic, and salt until smooth.

2. With the dough attachment or by hand, slowly add the flour and knead until the flour is well incorporated. If using a pasta machine, knead and cut into ¼-inch strips according to manufacturer's instructions. Spinach makes the dough sticky, so be sure to brush the dough with flour before passing it through the rollers of the machine. If processing by hand, knead the dough until it is smooth and elastic, about 8 minutes. Roll dough to desired thickness and cut into ¼-inch strips.

3. Dry the noodles for at least 30 minutes before cooking.

The noodles will dry best on a pasta rack. Clothes hangers are an effective substitute. Noodles can also be dried by spreading them out on cookie sheets and placing in a 200° oven for 10 minutes.

PESTO

½ cup olive oil
¾ cup pine nuts (or cashews), chopped
4 anchovies, mashed
2 scallions, white and green parts, finely chopped

½ cup minced garlic
1½ cups fresh basil, chopped (or ¾ cup dried)
1 teaspoon salt
½ teaspoon ground black pepper

In a skillet, heat the olive oil. Add all ingredients and cook over medium heat until the nuts are golden brown, 10 to 15 minutes. If the pesto seems too thick, add additional olive oil 1 tablespoon at a time.

Pesto can be stored in the refrigerator for several weeks.

SOUR CREAM CASHEW BREAD

2 packages dry yeast (½ ounce)
¼ cup honey
1¾ cups warm water (105-115°)
5 cups all-purpose flour
  (approximately)

1½ cups sour cream
1½ tablespoons salt
1 teaspoon baking soda
1 cup cashews, coarsely
  ground or chopped
Egg wash

1. Stir the yeast and honey into the warm water. Let stand until the yeast is soft and the mixture begins to foam, 3 to 5 minutes.

2. In a mixing bowl, combine the yeast mixture and 1 cup of flour. Add the sour cream, salt, and baking soda. Add additional flour, 1 cup at a time, mixing well to incorporate before adding more flour. After adding 2 cups of flour, stir in the cashews. Add the final cup of flour gradually until the dough is thick and comes away cleanly from the sides of the bowl.

3. Turn out onto a well-floured surface and knead until the dough is firm and elastic, 3 to 5 minutes. Place in an oiled bowl, cover with a clean cloth, and let rise until doubled, about 45 minutes, in a warm (80-85°) place.

4. Punch down the dough and turn out onto work surface. Divide into 3 equal pieces. Shape each piece of dough into a ball and place on a large baking sheet which has been greased and floured or covered with parchment paper. Brush with egg wash and let rise until doubled, 25 to 30 minutes. Bake at 350° for 30 to 40 minutes, or until top of bread is golden brown and the loaves sound hollow when tapped on the bottom.

Yogurt may be substituted for the sour cream. Hulled sunflower seeds, sprouted wheat, or any combination of nuts and/or seeds may be substituted for the cashews. This is a high altitude recipe. For elevations below 4,000 feet, decrease flour by ½ cup, decrease water by ¼ cup, and increase honey by 1 teaspoon.

PEACH RASPBERRY PIE

2 cups plus 3 tablespoons flour	4 peaches, peeled and pitted
½ cup plus 1 tablespoon sugar	¼ cup raspberries, halved
1 tablespoon cinnamon	1 tablespoon apple juice
¼ pound butter, chilled	1 tablespoon peach juice
¼ cup ice water	¼ cup raspberries, whole

1. In a bowl or on a work surface, combine 2 cups of flour, 1 tablespoon sugar, and the cinnamon. Cut in the butter until the mixture resembles the consistency of ground meal. Slowly add the ice water, mixing with a fork or fingers until the dough holds together. Form the dough into a ball, flatten slightly, cover with plastic wrap, and refrigerate 30 minutes.

2. Roll out the dough on a well-floured surface to fit a 9-inch pie tin. Dough will be ⅛ to ¼-inch thick. Press into the pie tin, flute edges, and refrigerate 30 minutes. Prick the bottom of the dough, cover with wax paper or aluminum foil, and fill with rice, beans, or pie weights. Bake until brown in 425° oven, 10 to 12 minutes. Turn off the oven. Remove the wax paper or foil and weights. Return the crust to the oven to dry completely while making the filling.

3. Cut 3 of the peaches into slices or small pieces. In a bowl, combine the peaches with ½ cup sugar, 3 tablespoons of flour, the raspberry halves, and the apple and peach juice. Stir gently to combine well.

4. Pour the filling into the baked shell. Slice the remaining peach into thin slices and arrange, slightly overlapping, around the perimeter of the pie. Distribute whole raspberries in the center. Sprinkle the surface with sugar. Bake at 350° for 30 minutes. Cover the crust with aluminum foil, increase temperature to 375°, and bake 10 more minutes. Serve while still slightly warm.

The pie will be juicy, so it should be served as soon as possible. Additional flour can be added to thicken the filling, but at the expense of the fresh fruit flavor.

GOLDEN CLIFF CHEESECAKE

CRUST:
1 *cup graham cracker crumbs*
⅓ *cup sugar*

½ *cup almonds, chopped*
 (or filberts or pecans)
¼ *cup butter, melted*

Combine all ingredients. Press to cover the bottom of a 10-inch springform pan that has been greased or covered with parchment. Bake at 325° for 5 minutes or until browned.

BOTTOM LAYER FILLING:
2½ *pounds cream cheese*
 (Philadelphia brand)
½ *cup sour cream*

1½ *cups sugar*
1 *tablespoon vanilla extract*
 Grated zest of 1 lemon

In an electric mixer, beat the cream cheese and sour cream at medium speed until smooth. Add remaining ingredients and beat at high speed for 1 minute. Pour mixture over baked crust, smooth with a spatula dipped in warm water, and bake for 20 minutes at 325°. The top of the layer must not brown or it will mar the appearance of the cake when cut. If the top begins to brown, remove at once. As soon as the bottom layer is finished baking, add the top layer filling.

TOP LAYER FILLING:
1 *cup sour cream*
1 *cup yogurt*

½ *cup sugar*
½ *teaspoon vanilla extract*
1 *tablespoon almond extract*

Mix all ingredients and spread on the bottom layer of the cake. Smooth the top carefully with a spatula dipped in warm water. Bake 10 minutes at 325°. Turn off the oven but do not remove the cake for another 10 minutes. Cool and refrigerate for at least 24 hours before removing from the pan and serving. The top of the cake will appear thin after baking but will set when chilled.

DEEP POWDER PUNCH

For each person:
1½ ounces brandy
1½ ounces vodka
¾ ounce light creme de cacao

½ ounce white creme de menthe
½ ounce cream of coconut
2 ounces heavy (whipping) cream
2 scoops cracked ice

Blend all ingredients thoroughly. Pour into a large, 17-ounce brandy snifter. If available, add 2 swizzle sticks in the shape of skis to suggest a skier fallen in deep powder snow.

GOLDEN WOK RESTAURANT

Dinner for Six

Fried Milk Pudding

Shrimp Balls

Sizzling Wor Bak Soup

Treasures in a Love Nest

Cabbage with Three Mushrooms

Chicken with Walnuts

Hong Siu Yellow Fish

Wine:

Rutherford Hill Gewürztraminer, 1982

David Lee, Ricky Lee, James Lui, Kam Wong Kwok, Owners

Sun Lee, Owner-Chef

For Sun Lee, a wok is an extension of arm and hand. As he quickly and nimbly maneuvers between work counter and wok stove, it is apparent that his culinary skills are second-nature if not truly innate. The movements with whisk, ladle, and strainer are swift and sure; multiple ingredients are added to the smoking wok with blinding speed and uncanny precision; the hot water splashes, the stiff brush scrubs, and the wok again awaits Lee's Midas touch.

Mandarin, Szechuan, Hunan, and Cantonese dishes comprise the extensive Golden Wok menu, but the house specialty is the cuisine of Lee's home province. Born in Canton, Lee, at age 16, learned the art and style of Chinese cooking in Hong Kong. He established a cooking reputation in London, New York City, and Chicago before coming to Salt Lake City in 1979. After cooking for two other local restaurants, Lee opened the Golden Wok in 1982 in West Valley City. In 1984 Golden Wok II opened in Salt Lake City.

Sun Lee personally presides over the kitchen at Golden Wok II. Like all talented chefs, he constantly tries to raise the American public's expectations of Chinese cuisine. In addition to many commonplace American favorites such as Mu Shu Pork, Lemon Chicken, and Won Ton Soup, the menu offers unusual Chinese delights such as Sizzling Curry Ox Tongue, Singapore Rice Noodles, Mongolian Chicken, and Salt Baked Shrimp. Lee also tries to bridge the cuisines of East and West with such specialty items as Emperor Pork Chops and Pepper Steak with Soy Bean Chicken. Vegetables, given a prominent place in Lee's dishes, are treated with serious respect. Lee also makes the most of local, seasonal produce: Honeydew Melon Chicken with Fresh Pineapple is a summer favorite. And he is willing, even eager, to accept on-the-spot as well as call-ahead requests for special dishes. If the ingredients are available, Sun Lee will prepare it—from sea cucumbers to pickled duck feet. In fact, many regular customers, impressed by his creativity (to wit, his own Fried Milk Pudding), simply order "whatever Mr. Lee recommends tonight." They are never disappointed.

Golden Wok I	Golden Wok II
2584 West 4700 South	420 East 3300 South
West Valley City	Salt Lake City
966-1421	486-4050

FRIED MILK PUDDING

1 tablespoon cornstarch	½ teaspoon salt
¼ cup milk	¼ teaspoon MSG (optional)
½ cup plus 1 teaspoon oil	1 teaspoon sugar
2 tablespoons butter	½ cup flour
1 cup chicken stock (see index)	¼ teaspoon baking soda
¼ cup canned coconut milk	½ cup water
	4 cups oil for frying

1. Combine the cornstarch and the milk. Reserve.

2. In a wok or saucepan over medium high heat, combine ½ cup oil and butter. When the butter has melted, add the chicken stock, coconut milk, salt, MSG, and sugar. Stir to combine thoroughly. Add cornstarch-milk mixture and stir constantly, preferably with a wire whisk, until the liquid thickens to the consistency of white gravy, about 3 to 4 minutes. Add more cornstarch if necessary. Pour the mixture into a greased 8- or 9-inch square pan. Cool and refrigerate overnight.

3. Thoroughly combine the flour, baking soda, water, and teaspoon of oil.

4. Cut the cold pudding into rectangles 1½-inches long and ½- to ¾-inch wide.

5. Heat 4 cups of oil in a wok to deep-fry temperature. Dip the pieces of milk pudding into the batter, taking care to coat each piece completely. Deep fry in batches until light brown, about 60 seconds.

The contrast in textures between the crispy coating and the creamy center makes Sun Lee's unique creation a most memorable appetizer. Although dairy products are not normally a part of Chinese cuisine, Guangdong Province, especially Daliang (Phoenix City), is famous for dishes made from the milk of the water buffalo.

SHRIMP BALLS

1 pound shrimp, shelled, deveined, and minced to a smooth paste	½ teaspoon salt
	¼ teaspoon MSG (optional)
	½ teaspoon sugar
2 water chestnuts, finely minced	4 cups oil for frying
	3 tablespoons cornstarch

1. Thoroughly combine all ingredients except oil and cornstarch. Grasp a handful of the shrimp mixture. Squeeze between the base of the thumb and the index finger to form a walnut-sized ball. Pinch off the shrimp ball. Repeat this process with the remaining shrimp mixture.

2. In a wok, heat the 4 cups of oil to deep-frying temperature. Roll 6 to 8 of the shrimp balls in the cornstarch, shaking off excess. Deep fry until they float to the surface of the oil and turn golden brown, 3 to 4 minutes. Drain the shrimp balls and place in a warm oven while frying those remaining. Makes about 24 shrimp balls.

The use of monosodium glutamate (MSG) in Chinese cooking is controversial. There is a long tradition in Chinese cuisine of using "taste powder," a soybean extract, to enhance flavor. Use of the modern chemical substitute MSG, also marketed under the brand-name Accent, is shunned by gastronomic purists who decry the use of artificial products and by persons who have an allergic reaction to the compound. Although most Chinese restaurants continue to use small amounts of MSG in preparing food, the ingredient is optional. If MSG is not used, add an additional pinch of salt.

SIZZLING WOR BAK SOUP

4 ounces pea pods,
   cut into 1-inch pieces
4 ears baby corn, cut into
   ⅛-inch thick rounds
1 cup shredded Chinese or
   Napa cabbage
½ chicken breast, diced
¼ pound lean pork, shredded
¼ pound baby shrimp, halved
12 bay scallops
2 teaspoons oil
1 tablespoon rice wine or
   dry sherry

4 cups chicken stock (see index)
½ teaspoon salt
¼ teaspoon MSG (optional)
1 teaspoon sugar
   Pinch of white pepper
2 tablespoons cornstarch dissolved in 2 tablespoons water
½ teaspoon soy sauce
   Sesame oil to taste
2 cups oil for frying
6 pieces Wor Bak
   (dried rice patties)

1. Blanch the vegetables, chicken, pork, shrimp, and scallops in boiling water for 60 seconds. Drain. Reserve.

2. In a wok or pot, bring the 2 teaspoons of oil, wine or sherry, chicken stock, salt, MSG, sugar, and pepper to a boil. Reduce heat. Add the reserved vegetables, meat, and seafood. Add the cornstarch and soy sauce. Just before serving add a few drops of sesame oil to taste.

3. While the broth is heating, heat 2 cups of oil in a wok to deep-frying temperature. Add 2 or 3 pieces of Wor Bak at a time, deep frying until puffed and slightly browned, about 10 seconds. Drain.

4. Place 1 piece of fried Wor Bak in each soup bowl. Ladle in hot soup and let each person delight in the sound of the sizzling rice.

Wor Bak, dried rice patties, can be purchased in 2-inch square pieces in Oriental markets. The Wor Bak must be deep fried just prior to serving or they will loose their crunchiness and will not sizzle properly.

TREASURES IN A LOVE NEST

¾ pound baking potatoes or
   taro root
¼ cup flour (approximately)
5½ cups oil for frying
¾ cup Chinese or Napa cabbage,
   cut into bite-size pieces
¾ cup broccoli florets
8-10 snow peas
1 medium carrot, diced
3 ounces small shrimp,
   shelled and deveined

3 ounces roast pork, cut into
   bite-size pieces
3 ounces chicken breast, diced
1 clove garlic, minced
1 snow crab leg, cut into
   bite-size pieces
¼ teaspoon salt
¼ teaspoon MSG
½ teaspoon sugar
1 teaspoon rice wine or dry sherry
1 teaspoon cornstarch dissolved
   in 1 teaspoon water

1. Cut the potatoes into julienne strips, ⅛-inch thick and 3 to 4 inches long. Mix the potato strips with the flour. Arrange the potato strips in the shape of a bird's nest . Deep fry the nest in 4 cups of oil until golden brown, 5 to 6 minutes. Drain nest. Reserve.

2. Blanch the cabbage, broccoli, snow peas, and carrots in boiling water for 60 seconds. Refresh in cold water to retain color. Drain. Reserve.

3. Heat 1½ cups of oil in a wok. Add the shrimp, pork, and chicken and cook for 20 seconds. Drain. Reserve.

4. Pour off all but about 2 tablespoons of the oil. Add the garlic and stir fry for 10 seconds. Add the vegetables, shrimp, pork, chicken, and the crab. Stir. Add the salt, MSG, and sugar. Stir-fry for 30 seconds. Add the wine and the cornstarch. Stir-fry another 30 seconds.

5. To serve, pour the vegetable-meat mixture into the bird's nest and have guests help themselves to the treasures. If desired, the treasures can be divided among small, individual nests.

The literal name for the taro or potato container in Chinese is "bird's nest," but Sun Lee prefers "love nest" to signify the exciting union of visual and taste delights. Sun Lee also prefers the use of taro root, when available, instead of potatoes in making the nest. The nest can be made in one of two ways. First, arrange the potato strips in irregular, overlapping fashion (like the twigs of a bird's nest) in a large Chinese strainer. Place a second strainer of equal or slightly smaller size on top of the potato strips and deep fry.

Second, punch 8 to 10 holes in the bottom of an aluminum dish 2 inches deep and 6 inches in diameter. Arrange potato strips as above. Use a strainer or large ladle to hold strips in place while deep frying. Specially designed wire baskets can be purchased to make small, 3- to 4-inch nests.

CABBAGE WITH THREE MUSHROOMS

3 ounces dried black mushrooms
3 ounces canned oyster
    mushrooms
3 ounces canned straw
    mushrooms
½ pound Chinese or Napa cabbage
2 tablespoons oil
½ teaspoon salt
1 clove garlic, minced

1 teaspoon rice wine or
    dry sherry
2 teaspoons oyster sauce
¼ teaspoon MSG (optional)
½ teaspoon sugar
⅛ teaspoon white pepper
1 teaspoon soy sauce
1 teaspoon cornstarch dissolved
    in 1 teaspoon water
¼ teaspoon sesame oil

1. Reconstitute the dried mushroms by soaking in warm water for 30 minutes. Squeeze to remove excess water. Cut away hard stems. Drain the canned mushrooms. Reserve all mushrooms.

2. Cut the cabbage into bite-size pieces. Blanch for 30 seconds in boiling water. Drain.

3. Heat 1 tablespoon of oil in a wok until smoking. Add the cabbage and ¼ teaspoon salt. Stir fry for 15 seconds. Transfer to a serving platter.

4. Heat 1 tablespoon of oil in the wok until smoking. Add the garlic, wine or sherry, oyster sauce, ¼ teaspoon salt, MSG, and sugar. Stir to combine. Add the mushrooms and stir. Add the white pepper and soy sauce. Stir. Add the cornstarch and sesame oil. Quickly stir to combine. Pour the mushrooms on top of the cabbage and serve.

Broccoli, green beans, snow peas, or any other green vegetable in season may be substituted for the cabbage or used in combination. The blanching time will vary with the vegetable to produce a crisp-tender texture. It is essential that fresh vegetables not be overcooked as the contrast between crunchy and soft textures is a hallmark of Chinese cuisine.

CHICKEN WITH WALNUTS

8 snow peas,
  cut into 1-inch pieces
¼ cup diced celery
¼ cup diced carrots
½ chicken breast,
  diced (about 1 cup)
2 cups oil for cooking
1 clove garlic, minced
¼ teaspoon salt

¼ teaspoon sugar
¼ teaspoon MSG (optional)
1 teaspoon oyster sauce
1 teaspoon rice wine or
  dry sherry
1 teaspoon cornstarch dissolved
  in 1 teaspoon water
⅓ cup walnut halves
  Sesame oil

1. Blanch the snow peas, celery, and carrots in boiling water for 30 seconds. Refresh in cold water to retain color. Drain. Reserve.

2. Heat the oil in a wok. Cook the chicken until the flesh turns from pink to white, about 20 seconds. Remove the chicken. Reserve.

3. Pour off the cooking oil, retaining about 2 tablespoons in the wok. Heat until smoking. Add the garlic and stir-fry for 10 seconds. Add the vegetables, salt, sugar, MSG, and oyster sauce. Stir-fry for 15 seconds. Add the chicken and wine. Stir to combine. Add the cornstarch. Stir to combine. Add the walnuts and a few drops of sesame oil to taste. Stir. Serve immediately.

HONG SIU YELLOW FISH

1 (1½-2 pound) whole yellow
  fish or sea bass
Flour
3 cups oil
12 (1-inch) cubes bean curd
1 clove garlic, minced
3 scallions, green and white parts,
  cut into 1-inch lengths
1 slice ginger (size and thickness
  of quarter), finely shredded

3 dried black mushrooms,
  reconstituted and sliced
1 teaspoon salt
½ teaspoon MSG (optional)
1 teaspoon sugar
3 ounces roast pork, shredded
1 cup chicken stock (see index)
2 teaspoons oyster sauce
Soy sauce to taste
1 tablespoon cornstarch dissolved in 1 tablespoon water

1. Clean and scale the fish leaving the head and tail attached. Coat lightly
   with flour and deep fry in the 3 cups of oil until nicely browned, about 5
   minutes per side. Remove to a warm serving platter.

2. Deep fry the bean curd cubes until browned, about 30 seconds. Reserve.

3. Pour off all but about 2 tablespoons of oil. Heat until smoking. Add the
   garlic, scallions, ginger, mushrooms, salt, MSG, and sugar. Stir-fry 10
   seconds. Add the pork, chicken stock, and oyster sauce. Cook until liquid begins to bubble. Add soy sauce to taste, 1 to 2 teaspoons. Add
   cornstarch and stir until the sauce is thickened and creamy. Pour over
   the fish and serve topped with bean curd.

*The presentation of a whole fish is a traditional finale to a Chinese meal as the
symbol of abundance. Although formal banquets often end with "sweets,"
Sun Lee does not serve desserts in keeping with the tradition of family dining.*

JAZ RANCH
Bistro

Dinner for Four

White Gazpacho with Balsamic Vinegar

Pizzette with Essence of Tomato, Singed Garlic, Tapénade, and Clams

Hearts of Caesar Salad

Chicken Wentletrap in the Thai Style

Butter Lime Rice

Utah Apricot Chèvre Ice Cream

Wines:

With the Pizzette—Sangiovese Dell Umbria, 1982
or
Vino Nobile de Montepulciano, Cantina del Redi, 1978

With the Chicken—Mark West, Russian River Valley Gewürtztraminer, 1983

With the Ice Cream—Non-Vintage Deutz, Ay-Champagne

Jacqueline Landeen, Owner-Chef

Thomas Hildebrand, Owner-Chef

Surprises to delight the palate and eye abound at the unusually but appropriately named Jaz Ranch Bistro. "Jaz" because Salt Lake is a progressive city with a strong jazz tradition—"but only one 'z' because the city is not frenetically progressive." "Ranch" because local farms and ranches supply most of the meats, dairy products, and produce used in the kitchen. "Bistro" because it is an unpretentious establishment that places a premium on good food and warm hospitality.

Although their cuisine is often called "new American" or "northern California nouvelle," Jacqueline Landeen and Thomas Hildebrand shun all labels other than "our own style of cooking." Essentially, the Jaz Ranch cuisine turns on the creative use of fresh, local, seasonal products along with an appropriate international blending of foods of the East and West. From Roast Suckling Pig with American Indian Sauce and Vegetarian Moussaka to fruit vinaigrettes and homemade triple cream cheeses, the dishes at the Jaz Ranch exhibit unique spicings and innovative food combinations. Although the menu at any given time is brief, there is extraordinary variety because the entire menu changes weekly and "no dish is ever repeated—not with the same sauce or garnishes or cooking method." There is much more to the cuisine than ingredients, techniques, and presentations. As Landeen explains: "Jaz Ranch's culinary integrity lies in food that is replete with passion and flavor, those essential ingredients that keep the human spirit glowing and constitute cuisine de Jaz."

The decor is an art deco dream. The copper and green ceilings and walls, done beautifully in the rare "trompe l'oeil" style, literally fool and trick the eye and thus contrast effectively with the plain wood floor. Dramatic flower arrangements add further interest to the unadorned yet inviting dining room. Warmth and personality abound at the Jaz Ranch—in the decor, in the cuisine, and in the friendly interaction between staff and patrons. Among the establishment's loyal following are many culinary celebrities—prominent amateur cooks and professional chefs intrigued by "what's cooking down at the Ranch."

147 West Broadway   355-2800
Salt Lake City

WHITE GAZPACHO WITH BALSAMIC VINEGAR

½ cup raw almonds
½ teaspoon salt
3 medium cloves garlic, peeled
3 slices day-old French style
   bread, baguette size,
   cut 1-inch thick

1 cup fresh squeezed
   orange juice
2 cups water
2 tablespoons balsamic vinegar
½ cup olive oil
28 green seedless grapes

1. Blanch the almonds for 15 seconds in boiling water. Remove the skins. Place the almonds on a baking sheet, sprinkle with the salt, and place under a broiler until golden.

2. In a food processor or blender, beat the almonds and garlic until the almonds are finely ground.

3. Soak the bread, crust removed, in the orange juice and water. Squeeze the bread to remove excess moisture. Add the bread to the food processor or blender and beat until well combined and smooth. Add the orange juice and water soaking mixture and beat 3 to 4 minutes.

4. Pour the soup into a large mixing bowl. Whisk in the balsamic vinegar. Add the olive oil and whisk to blend well. Chill. Rewhisk before serving.

5. Serve very cold, garnished with 7 grapes per serving.

In addition to the well known red gazpacho of Andalucia, Spain is also the home of two white gazpachos. One is a vegetable soup from Extremadura that omits tomatoes. The other is an almond and grape soup from Malaga. The green grapes are not decorative; their sweetness and textures are essential to the soup.

PIZZETTE with ESSENCE of TOMATO, SINGED GARLIC, TAPÉNADE, and CLAMS

32 *clams*
     PIZZETTE DOUGH
     Olive oil
     ESSENCE OF TOMATO

     SINGED GARLIC
     TAPÉNADE
½ *cup grated goat cheese*

1. Scrub and rinse the clams. Steam until shells open. Remove the clams from the shells and place in the steaming liquid until ready for use.

2. Divide the PIZZETE DOUGH into 4 balls, approximately 3 ounces each. Roll each ball into an 8-inch round approximately ⅛-inch thick (or as thin as possible). Place the rounds on baking sheets coated with olive oil.

3. Spread ¼ cup of ESSENCE OF TOMATO evenly over each pizzette. Scatter the SINGED GARLIC over the sauce. Arrange 8 clams around the perimeter of each pizzette. Top each clam with ¼ teaspoon of the TAPENADE. Sprinkle surface lightly with the grated goat cheese. Bake in a pre-heated 450° oven for 15 to 20 minutes, watching closely so that the pizzette does not burn. Remove from the oven when the bottom of the pizzette is crisp. Cut into wedges. Serve immediately

PIZZETTE DOUGH

1 *package dry yeast*
¼ *cup warm water (105-115°)*
1 *cup all-purpose flour*

¼ *teaspoon salt*
1 *tablespoon softened butter*

Dissolve the yeast in the warm water. Combine with the other ingredients and knead until the dough is smooth and elastic, 8 to 10 minutes. Cover and put in a warm place to rise for 2 hours.

ESSENCE OF TOMATO

2 pounds fresh tomatoes,
    chopped
½ teaspoon fresh ground
    black pepper

¼ teaspoon cinnamon
2 teaspoons sugar
1 tablespoon olive oil

Sauté the tomatoes with the seasonings in olive oil over medium high heat for 2 to 3 minutes. Reduce the heat, cover, and let stew until the liquid has reduced by half, 5 to 6 minutes. Pass through a strainer. If the sauce seems too thin, reduce further over medium heat.

SINGED GARLIC

5 medium cloves garlic,
    peeled and minced

2 tablespoons olive oil

Sauté the garlic in hot oil until brown and crisp, but not burned. Remove to a small bowl with the oil to keep the garlic moist and the pieces separated.

TAPÉNADE

1 cup black, pitted Mediterranean
    olives (Gaeta preferred)
½ cup olive oil
1 tin anchovies (2 ounces),
    rinsed and drained

2 tablespoons capers,
    rinsed and drained
1 tablespoon lemon juice
    Fresh cracked black pepper,
    about 4 twists
2 tablespoons brandy

Purée the olives and olive oil in a blender. Add the anchovies, capers, lemon juice, and pepper. Blend to a coarse paste. Add the brandy and continue blending to a smooth paste.

HEARTS OF CAESAR SALAD

4 *heads romaine lettuce*
¾ *cup olive oil*
1 *teaspoon finely chopped garlic*
  Juice of 1 lemon
⅛ *teaspoon sugar*
4 *anchovy filets*
2 *egg yolks*

4½ *teaspoons Worcestershire sauce*
4 *thin slices French style bread,*
  baguette style
1 *cup grated Romano cheese*
  (or Parmesan)
  Fresh cracked pepper to taste

1. Separate the outer leaves from the tender, inner hearts of the romaine. Reserve the outer leaves for future use. Wash the inner hearts in cold water, pat dry, and set aside.

2. Whisk together the olive oil, garlic, lemon juice, and sugar until well combined.

3. In a separate, large bowl, mash the anchovies thoroughly with a fork. Add the egg yolks and Worcestershire sauce. Mix well. Add the olive oil mixture and combine.

4. Toast the bread slices until crisp on both sides. Dip one side of each crouton in the dressing. Set aside.

5. Place the hearts of romaine on top of the dressing. Sprinkle with ⅔ cup of the cheese and fresh cracked black pepper to taste, about 15 twists. Using both hands, gently toss the hearts of romaine to coat with the dressing.

6. Arrange the hearts of romaine in a fan shape on individual plates. Sprinkle with the remaining cheese and top with a crouton.

The use of the hand is indispensable in preparing and eating a Caesar Salad. The process of hand-tossing the lettuce in the dressing is not an affectation. It actually coats the lettuce leaves much better than if the dressing was poured over the lettuce and tossed. And the traditional (and proper) way to eat a Caesar Salad is to pick up individual hearts of romaine with the fingers instead of cutting them with a knife or fork.

It is important that the anchovies be mashed to a smooth paste. Most people who dislike Caesar Salad actually object only to chunks of anchovies that do not blend into the dressing.

At the Jaz Ranch we use small Pee Wee eggs laid by young chickens instead of the regular grades of eggs laid by mature chickens and sold in supermarkets. Pee Wee eggs have much less membrane tissue than regular eggs and have lighter, clearer whites. We find that they make a noticeable difference in the smoothness of custards and ice creams. Also, Pee Wee egg shells produce a clearer stock. Two Pee Wee eggs are the equivalent of one "large" egg. Because Pee Wees are not widely available, all references to eggs in our recipes are to Grade AA "large" commercial eggs.

CHICKEN WENTLETRAP IN THE THAI STYLE

4 tablespoons fresh lime juice	6 scallions, white portion only cut in 1-inch lengths
4 tablespoons brown sugar	
¾ cup mushroom soy sauce	5 small jalapeño peppers, minced
4 whole chicken breasts	2 tablespoons minced ginger root
2 tablespoons butter	
2 tablespoons olive or vegetable oil	⅓ cup fresh basil leaves
	⅓ cup fresh mint leaves
8 small garlic cloves, pounded	LIME RICE
	¾ cup chopped roasted peanuts

1. Bring the lime juice, brown sugar, and mushroom soy sauce to a boil. Reduce heat and simmer for 10 minutes. Set aside.

2. Bone the chicken breasts. Place the breasts between pieces of plastic wrap and pound with a mallet until thin, about ⅛-inch thick. Roll the breasts lengthwise to resemble the shape of a conical sea shell or cornucopia. Securely tie with kitchen twine or string leaving 1-inch intervals along the length of the rolled breasts.

3. Melt 1 tablespoon of butter and 1 tablespoon of oil in a large skillet over high heat. Sear the chicken breasts until evenly browned, 2 to 3 minutes. Transfer to a preheated 350° oven and roast 9 to 10 minutes.

continued...

4. While the chicken is roasting, melt 1 tablespoon of butter and 1 tablespoon of oil over high heat in a wok or skillet. Add the garlic, scallion, jalapeño and ginger. Stir fry for 30 seconds. Add the reserved soy sauce mixture and simmer until the liquid is slightly reduced and thickened. Add the basil and mint leaves. Toss and remove from heat.

5. Spoon a serving of LIME RICE in the center of each plate. Remove the twine from the chicken and place the rolled breast on the rice. Pour the sauce over the chicken and top with the chopped peanuts.

Thai food should assault the taste buds with hot and spicy seasonings. Removing the seeds from the jalapeños will make the sauce less hot. Mushroom soy sauce is available in Oriental markets. A wentletrap is an elegant, white sea shell with circular "staircase" rings. The shape of the rolled chicken breast and the markings of the twine inspired the name of this dish.

LIME RICE

1 *cup white, long grain rice*	1 *tablespoon lime zest*
	1 *tablespoon butter*

Cook the rice according to manufacturer's instructions. Sauté the lime zest in the butter for 1 minute. Stir the lime zest and butter through the cooked rice.

UTAH APRICOT CHÈVRE ICE CREAM

2 *pounds fresh apricots*
2 *cups sugar*
3 *cups sparkling water*

1 *pound soft chèvre*
   (goat cheese)
2 *cups heavy (whipping) cream*
4 *eggs, room temperature*

1. Halve the apricots, remove the pits, but do not peel. Stew the unpeeled apricots along with the pits in the sugar and water until soft. Remove the pits and simmer until the liquid is reduced and coats the back of a wooden spoon. Pour the apricot mixture into the bowl of a food processor or blender, in batches if necessary, and blend at high speed until smooth. Chill.

2. In a food processor, pulse-blend the softened chevre with the chilled apricot mixture until smooth. Add 1 cup of the cream. Pulse-blend. Add the eggs, one at a time, blending well before adding the next egg. Remove to a large bowl and stir in the remaining 1 cup cream. Pour into the container of an electric ice cream maker and freeze according to manufacturer's instructions.

Peaches may be substituted for the apricots. Do not use tinned or frozen fruit. Because apricots and peaches are seasonal, we make homemade preserves for use throughout the year. Simply stew the apricots or peaches as in Step 1 of the recipe. Can instead of blending. Substitute 2½ cups of homemade preserves for the 2 pounds of fresh fruit. Commercial preserves will not work for this recipe.

Makes 2 quarts.

La Caille  at Quail Run

Dinner for Six

Salmon Rolls

Spinach Salad

Roast Duck with Orange Sauce

Anaheim Pepper Cornucopia

Croissants

Baked Alaska

Wines:

With the Salmon—Trimbach Pinot Gris, 1982

With the Duck—Grand Cru Sonoma Gewürztraminer, 1982

With the Baked Alaska—Phelps Napa Riesling, Late Harvest, 1980

David Johnson, Owner

Steve Runolfson, Owner

Mark L. Haug, General Manager and Chef

Opened in 1975 after three years of painstaking preparation and construction, La Caille at Quail Run is aptly described as "an island in time." Located at the mouth of Little Cottonwood Canyon, La Caille magically transports visitors to an eighteenth-century French country estate. The journey begins at the massive iron gates at the foot of the brick drive that winds through 20 lush acres containing gardens, orchards, vineyards, ponds, streams, walkways, and gazebos. Guests frequently join ducks, swans, and peafowl in roaming the grounds. The restaurant is housed in an imposing stone and stucco replica of a two-story farmhouse. Beamed ceilings, plank flooring, wooden tables and chairs, open-hearth fireplaces, an impressive collection of antiques, and costumed service personnel contribute to an atmosphere of rustic elegance.

The dream that is La Caille began in 1969 when Lester Johnson opened the original restaurant called Quail Run. The current owners, one of whom is Lester's son, and the general manager began their association with La Caille as teenaged kitchen help at the original restaurant. They are committed to the dual concept of change and self-sufficiency in the entire operation. Most of the herbs and many of the in-season fruits and vegetables used in the kitchen are grown on the grounds. A fully operational winery will soon process the first crush for La Caille wine made from French hybrid grapes grown in the vineyards.

La Caille can accommodate 248 guests for traditional French country cuisine Monday through Saturday and for brunch and a special Basque style family dinner on Sunday.

9565 Wasatch Boulevard   942-1751
Sandy

SALMON ROLLS

1 *pound fresh salmon*
2 *stalks celery, tops only*
¼ *small onion*
⅛ *teaspoon tarragon*
1 *clove garlic, finely minced*
¼ *cup finely chopped celery*
¼ *cup finely chopped onion,*
    sautéed until soft

½ *cup cooked white rice*
¼-⅓ *cup mayonnaise*
    Salt and white pepper to taste
½ *pound PUFF PASTRY*
1 *egg beaten with*
    1 tablespoon water
SALMON GLAZE
Parsley for garnish

1. Cook the salmon in 2 cups of water along with the tops of 2 stalks of celery and ¼ small onion until the salmon begins to flake, about 8 minutes. Remove the salmon. Discard aromatics. Over high heat reduce cooking liquid by half, approximately 1 cup. Strain. Reserve salmon stock.

2. Remove the skin and bones from the salmon. Mix thoroughly with the tarragon, garlic, celery, onion, and rice. Add enough mayonnaise to bind ingredients into a texture similar to tuna salad. Add salt and white pepper to taste.

3. Roll PUFF PASTRY into a rectangle about 12 x 4 and ⅛-inch thick. With a spoon or a pastry bag fitted with a 1-inch tip, form the salmon mixture into a 1-inch cylinder running lengthwise down the center of the dough. Fold the dough around the mixture, sealing seam and ends with egg wash. Place seam-side down on a lightly greased baking sheet. Brush with egg wash and bake at 400° until pastry is golden brown, 25 to 30 minutes.

4. To serve, cut Salmon Roll into slices of preferred thickness. Top and surround with SALMON GLAZE. Garnish with a sprig of parsley.

PUFF PASTRY

2 tablespoons lard or shortening
1¾ cups flour

½ cup water (approximately)
2 tablespoons lemon juice
6 ounces margarine or butter

1. In a mixing bowl, cut the lard into the flour. Add the liquids. Knead for 10 minutes by hand or 6 to 7 minutes with a dough hook until the dough is smooth and well developed. Turn onto a floured surface and let rest 10 minutes.
2. Roll the dough into a rectangle about 12 x 8-inches. Leaving a margin of about 1 inch around the edges, spread the margarine over ⅔ of the dough. Fold uncovered side over, brush off excess flour, and fold over remaining third so that you have layers of dough/margarine/dough/margarine/dough. Let rest 10 minutes.
3. Turn dough a quarter turn and roll to original size. Fold both ends to the middle like a book. Brush off excess flour. Fold halves together. Let rest 10 minutes.
4. Repeat Step 3 two more times.
5. Turn dough a quarter turn. Roll to original size. Fold in thirds as in Step 2. Refrigerate for at least 24 hours before using.

This recipe makes 1 pound of puff dough. Puff dough can be refrigerated for up to 1 week or frozen for up to 3 months. Butter may be used instead of margarine. If using butter, let the dough rest in the refrigerator between rollings.

SALMON GLAZE

1 cup salmon stock
¼ cup dry sherry
3 tablespoons tomato purée or sauce

½ small green bell pepper
⅛ teaspoon ham bouillon powder
⅛ teaspoon chicken bouillon powder
Cornstarch as needed

Combine the first six ingredients in a saucepan, bring to a boil, and simmer 10 to 15 minutes. Add cornstarch dissolved in water to thicken slightly; glaze should be thin but not runny.

SPINACH SALAD

10 strips bacon, cut into
    julienne strips
4 bunches spinach, leaves
    washed and dried

DIJON VINAIGRETTE
3 hard boiled eggs, diced

1. Fry bacon strips until crisp. Remove the bacon with a slotted spoon. Reserve fat.

2. Transfer the bacon to a large, stainless steel bowl or pot. Add the spinach and DIJON VINAIGRETTE. Toss gently over high heat until the spinach leaves are slightly wilted and the salad is hot. Add the bacon fat and toss another 15 to 20 seconds. Serve immediately garnished with diced eggs.

DIJON VINAIGRETTE

1 tablespoon grated Romano
    cheese
¼ cup tarragon vinegar
¼ cup mayonnaise
8 tablespoons Dijon mustard
1½ tablespoons sugar

⅛ teaspoon each salt, paprika,
    garlic salt, celery seeds,
    poppy seeds, sesame seeds,
    and black pepper
1 cup vegetable oil

Combine all ingredients except the oil in a mixing bowl or blender. Slowly blend while adding oil in a thin, steady stream.

ROAST DUCK WITH ORANGE SAUCE

3 ducklings	Ground black pepper
Tarragon	ORANGE SAUCE
Salt	Orange segments for garnish

1. Halve the ducklings and bone except for the last joint in the leg. Reserve bones for stock.
2. Place the duck halves, skin side up, in a large roasting pan. Sprinkle with tarragon, salt, and pepper. Roast in a hot (450°) oven until the duck is completely cooked and the skin is nicley browned, about 30 minutes.
3. Serve ½ duckling per person covered with ORANGE SAUCE and garnished with orange segments.

ORANGE SAUCE

1 cup DUCK STOCK	⅛ teaspoon each thyme, basil, tarragon, and chervil
½ cup dry white wine	1 teaspoon cider vinegar
½ cup beer	2 tablespoons brandy
2 tablespoons sugar	1½ cups (12-ounces) frozen orange juice concentrate
2 tablespoons honey	Cornstarch as needed
1 bay leaf	

1. Bring the stock, wine, and beer to a boil and cook at a boil for 5 minutes to remove the alcohol.
2. While the liquid is boiling, cook the sugar over high heat, stirring constantly, until caramelized. Add a little water while cooking to prevent sugar from setting.
3. Add the caramelized sugar, honey, and herbs to the stock. Cook 5 minutes over medium heat, stirring frequently. Add the vinegar, brandy, and orange juice. Bring to a boil for 5 minutes. Add the cornstarch dissolved in water until the sauce is thick but still pourable.

LA CAILLE AT QUAIL RUN

DUCK STOCK

Bones from 3 ducklings
8 cups water

3 cups dry white wine
1 onion
1 tomato

Place the duck bones in a roasting pan and brown in a hot (450°) oven for 20 minutes. Transfer browned bones to a stock pot with the other ingredients. Boil until the stock is reduced by half, about 5 cups. Strain. Duck stock can be stored in the refrigerator 2 to 3 days or frozen for several months.

ANAHEIM PEPPER CORNUCOPIA

6 *Anaheim green peppers*	12 *Enoki mushrooms*
12 *julienne strips snow peas*	12 *pieces fresh chives*
12 *julienne strips red bell pepper*	*Oil, preferably peanut oil,*
12 *julienne strips zucchini*	*for frying*
12 *julienne strips yellow squash*	*Salt and pepper*

1. Cut the stem end of the Anaheim peppers on the diagonal to resemble a cornucopia. Scoop out seeds and veins. Steam peppers 4 to 5 minutes. Remove skins.

2. Briefly stir-fry remaining vegetables until crisp-tender. Sprinkle with salt and pepper.

3. Fill each Anaheim pepper with 2 julienne strips of each vegetable; the ends of the vegetables should stick out of the cornucopia.

CROISSANTS

2 packages dry yeast
1 cup warm milk
2 eggs, room temperature
2 tablespoons sugar

2 teaspoons salt
3-4 cups flour
¾ pound margarine
1 egg beaten with 1 tablespoon water

1. Sprinkle the yeast over the milk in a mixing bowl, stir, and let set 5 to 10 minutes. Stir the eggs, sugar, and salt into the yeast mixture. Add 3 cups of flour, 1 cup at a time, mixing well to incorporate. Add the remaining flour ¼ cup at a time until the dough reaches a soft consistency and pulls away cleanly from the sides of the bowl.

2. Turn the dough onto a well-floured surface. Roll the dough into a rectangle about 8 x 10 inches. Spread margarine over the surface of the dough leaving a ½-inch margin around the edges. Fold in thirds, as a letter, brushing off excess flour. Fold the dough in half, top to bottom. Turn a quarter turn.

3. Repeat rolling and folding as in Step 2.

4. Repeat rolling and folding as in Step 2.

5. Roll to a rectangle of the original size. Cut the dough in half. Place one half on top of the other half. Wrap in plastic wrap and refrigerate for 1 hour.

6. Roll out the dough to a thickness of ⅛-inch. Using a pizza cutter or knife, cut the dough into isosceles triangles 5 x 7 x 7. Roll the triangles from the short side to the tip. Turn the ends slightly toward the center to resemble a crescent. Brush croissants with the egg wash. Let rise until almost doubled, about 45 minutes. Bake in 350° oven 25 to 30 minutes or until well-browned.

Butter may be substituted for margarine. If butter is used, refrigerate 30 minutes after Steps 2, 3, and 4. Croissants freeze well for several months.

BAKED ALASKA

1 WHITE CAKE	8 egg whites
½ pint strawberry ice cream	½ cup sugar
½ pint chocolate ice cream	¼ cup brandy (optional)
½ pint vanilla ice cream	

1. Line a 6-inch diameter bowl with plastic wrap. Cut the cake into 1-inch thick slices. Line the bowl with cake slices, pressing as necessary to line the bowl completely. Fill with alternate layers of strawberry, chocolate, and vanilla ice cream. Cover the top layer of ice cream with cake pieces. Invert the bowl onto a baking sheet or oven-proof serving plate. Remove the bowl and peel off the plastic wrap.

2. Make a meringue by beating the egg whites until the soft peak stage. Add the sugar and continue beating until it reaches the stiff peak stage.

3. Cover the entire cake with meringue. Using the tip of a spatula, form peaks of meringue at regular intervals around the entire surface of the cake.

4. Bake in a 450° oven for 5 to 6 minutes or until tips of the meringue peaks turn golden brown.

5. Serve immediately. Flambé with brandy if desired.

It is essential to cover the entire surface of the cake with meringue as it serves as insulation to keep the ice cream from melting.

WHITE CAKE

1 cup milk	1½ cups sugar
¾ cup shortening	2¼ cups sifted cake flour
1 teaspoon salt	3 teaspoons baking powder
½ teaspoon vanilla	5 egg whites, lightly beaten

1. In an electric mixer or by hand, thoroughly combine the milk, shortening, salt, vanilla, and sugar. Sift the flour and baking powder together and add to the batter. Blend well. Fold in the egg whites.

2. Pour the batter into a greased and floured 9 x 11-inch square cake pan. Bake at 375° for 18 to 20 minutes. Remove the cake from the pan and cool on a wire rack.

Any white or yellow cake, packaged or homemade, will work for Baked Alaska.

Dinner for Six

Les Champignons Café de Paris

La Salade D'Epinards Flambé

Veau Normandie

Les Légumes

La Mousse au Chocolat

Grand Marnier Café

Wine:

Trimbach Riesling, 1980
or
Mumm's Champagne

Margueritte Gales, Owner-Chef

Roman Gales, Owner-Chef

LA FLEUR DE LYS

Amidst the bustle of the downtown business section, the quietude of old world atmosphere beckons diners to the garden level of Arrow Press Square. Serenity and elegance in a French parlor setting describe the atmosphere and decor of La Fleur de Lys. Needlepoint tapestries, velvet and brocade settees, classical music, and candlelight add to the intimate, European ambiance.

The opening of the original La Fleur de Lys in 1973 heralded the beginning of a dining revolution in Salt Lake City. La Fleur was not only the city's first exclusive French restaurant, but also the first restaurant to offer haute cuisine in the grand tradition—gourmet food accompanied by bone china, crystal, and sterling silver table service.

Presiding over the inner working of La Fleur are Margueritte Gales, who took over the restaurant in 1976, and her son, Roman. Alsatian-born Margueritte literally grew up in the kitchen, learning the fine points of French cuisine from an uncle, a Cordon Bleu graduate, who operated a hotel and restaurant in Luxembourg. Fittingly, Roman attributes his decision to continue the family tradition of restaurateurs to "Mother's influence and talent." To the Gales, La Fleur is more a way of life than a business. "We would be happy to have all 60 seats filled and not turn over a single table during the evening. We want our guests to enjoy our attentive service and have a leisurely, memorable dining experience."

La Fleur features classic French cuisine with a modern touch. The influence of la nouvelle cuisine is evident in the preparation and presentation of food with as light a hand as possible. The health conscious proprietors use very little salt and no artificial products. "There is no margarine in the kitchen," boasts Margueritte. Only the freshest and highest quality ingredients are acceptable in "the French restaurant without compromise."

165 South West Temple   359-5753
Salt Lake City

LES CHAMPIGNONS CAFÉ DE PARIS

¼ *pound butter, clarified*
30 *large mushrooms,*
   cleaned and stemmed

Salt and white pepper to taste
GARLIC BUTTER

1. Melt the butter in a sauté pan over medium-low heat. Place the mushrooms, tops down, in the butter, sprinkle with salt and pepper, and sauté for 2 minutes. Turn the mushrooms, sprinkle with salt and pepper, and sauté, turning occasionally, for 3 to 4 minutes or until mushrooms are tender.

2. Melt the GARLIC BUTTER in a chafing dish or other heat-proof serving container with a lid. Place the mushrooms in the dish, tops up, cover, and heat until steaming, 1 to 2 minutes.

3. Bring the dish to the table before removing the lid so that guests can enjoy the heady aroma of the GARLIC BUTTER. Serve 5 mushrooms per person, liberally drenched in GARLIC BUTTER. Accompany with French bread for dipping in the GARLIC BUTTER.

Individual casseroles with lids would be ideal for this dish. Casseroles can be put in a hot oven to steam before serving.

GARLIC BUTTER

6 *large cloves garlic*
1 *small onion*
½ *bunch parsley, leaves only*
1 *pound butter,*
   room temperature

2 *teaspoons lemon juice*
   (approximately)
1 *tablespoon dry white wine*
   (approximately)
Salt and white pepper

In a food processor or with a sharp knife, very finely mince the garlic, onion, and parsley. Combine with the butter in a mixing bowl and blend thoroughly. Add the lemon juice, wine, salt, and pepper to taste.

The amount of seasoning necessary for the butter will vary considerably depending upon the taste of the garlic and onion. Garlic butter will keep for several weeks in the refrigerator and can be used as a delightful seasoning for many dishes, especially seafood.

LA SALADE D'EPINARDS FLAMBÉ

5 slices bacon,
　crisp fried and chopped
3 tablespoons sugar
2½ tablespoons Worcestershire
　sauce
¼ cup Cognac or other brandy

1½ cups SAUCE VINAIGRETTE
4 bunches spinach, leaves
　washed and torn into
　bite-size pieces
Juice of 1 lemon
Fresh ground pepper to taste

1. Sauté the bacon, sugar, and Worcestershire sauce over medium heat until bubbling. Add Cognac and flambé. When the flame has burned out, add the VINAIGRETTE and bring to a boil, stirring occasionally.

2. Put the spinach leaves in a large salad bowl, sprinkle with lemon juice, and toss. Pour the sauce over the spinach. Keep the bowl covered as much as possible with the pan while tossing the spinach and sauce in order to concentrate aroma and flavor. Season with fresh ground pepper. Serve immediately.

SAUCE VINAIGRETTE

2 egg yolks
3 tablespoons Dijon mustard
2 cups oil

⅓ cup red wine vinegar
¼ teaspoon salt
⅛ teaspoon white pepper

In a large bowl, beat the egg yolks and the mustard with a wire whisk to blend well. While whisking, add the oil in a thin, steady stream. Whisk briskly until the mixture reaches the consistency of thin mayonnaise. Add the vinegar, salt, and pepper. Blend. Adjust seasonings.

VEAU NORMANDIE

2 *pounds veal loin, cut into*
   1-inch medallions
   Flour
   Salt and white pepper
¼ *pound butter, clarified*

3 *teaspoons chopped shallots*
6 *large mushrooms, cleaned,*
   trimmed, and sliced
½ *cup Cognac or other brandy*
1½ *cups heavy (whipping) cream*

1. Pound the veal medallions with a mallet between pieces of plastic wrap until ⅛-inch thick.
2. Lightly flour the medallions and sprinkle with salt and white pepper. Sauté in a large pan in 2 to 3 tablespoons butter over medium-low heat, turning once, until the edges of the veal just begin to brown, about 1 minute total. Do not brown or overcook the veal. Remove to a heated platter and place in a warm oven while making the sauce.
3. Sauté the shallots and mushrooms in the remaining butter over medium heat until shallots are soft and translucent. Add the Cognac and ignite. When the flame is extinguished, add the cream. Increase the heat and let the cream reduce until thick enough so that the sauce will not run off of the meat. Adjust seasonings.
4. Serve 4 to 5 medallions per person topped with cream sauce.

If possible, coordinate cooking by sautéing veal and making the cream sauce simultaneously in separate skillets.

LES LEGUMES

2 medium carrots, peeled and
    cut into julienne strips
2 tablespoons butter
30-36 snow pea pods (5-6 per person)
1 teaspoon sugar

Salt and white pepper to taste
3 tomatoes
Dried or fresh basil,
    finely chopped

1. Blanch the carrots in boiling water until just *al dente*.

2. In a skillet melt the butter over medium heat. Add the carrots, snow peas, sugar, and sprinkle with salt and pepper. Sauté 3 to 4 minutes until the snow peas are crisp-tender.

3. While the carrots and snow peas are cooking, cut the tomatoes in half. Remove stem ends. Sprinkle halves with fresh or dried basil. Bake in a hot (400°) oven 3 to 4 minutes.

4. Serve the three vegetables with the entrée arranged attractively on the plate.

LA MOUSSE AU CHOCOLAT

10 ounces semi-sweet chocolate
½ pound butter
¼ cup Triple Sec or other
    orange liqueur

8 eggs, separated
½ cup sugar
1 pint heavy (whipping) cream

1. Melt the chocolate, butter, and Triple Sec in the top of a double boiler. Stir to incorporate. Let cool.

2. In an electric mixer, beat the egg yolks and sugar at high speed until the mixture forms a ribbon when the beaters are raised, about 10 minutes.

3. In a large bowl, combine the chocolate sauce with the egg mixture. Beat with a wire whisk until thick.

4. In another bowl, beat the egg whites with a whisk until stiff peaks form. Using a spatula, fold the egg whites into the chocolate sauce until just combined.

5. Whisk the whipping cream vigorously with a wire whisk until thick. Fold, using a spatula, into the chocolate-egg whites mixture. Chill for at least 3 hours before serving. The mousse will hold 3 to 4 days refrigerated.

GRAND MARNIER CAFÉ

½ *lemon, quartered*
½-⅔ *cup sugar*
1½ *ounces brandy*

9 *ounces Grand Marnier*
    Strong, hot coffee
1 *cup heavy cream, whipped*

1. Circle the rims of 6 heat-proof glasses with a lemon wedge.

2. Put the sugar on a saucer and coat the rims of the glasses as for a Margarita.

3. Divide the brandy (about ¼ ounce) and Grand Marnier (about 1½ ounces) among the glasses and ignite, swirling the glasses so that the burning liquor lightly caramelizes the sugar.

4. Add coffee while the liquor is still flaming. Top with a dollop of whipped cream and drizzle with additional Grand Marnier.

The addition of brandy is to help ignition. Warming the glasses after the liquor has been added will also facilitate ignition. Irish whiskey, Galliano, and Amaretto are popular substitutes for Grand Marnier.

Dinner for Six

Seafood Cocktail

Lentil Soup

Braised Lamb Shanks

Rice Pilaf

French Fried Zucchini

Rice Pudding

Wine:

With the Lamb—Guenoc Lake County Petite Sirah, 1981

The Speros Family, Owners

Jerry Sanchez, Chef

It is hard to say what is most appealing about Lamb's—the extensive menu featuring "home cooking," the comfortable surroundings and superb service, the convivial atmosphere of Salt Lake's busiest restaurant, or the solid family tradition of the venerable Main Street establishment. Actually, it is the sum of these parts and even more that explains the enduring popularity of Utah's oldest family-owned restaurant.

George Lamb opened the original restaurant in Logan in 1919. When he moved the restaurant to its present location in the historic Herald Building in 1939, Ted Speros left the copper mines to join Lamb in the business. Today the Speros family, which assumed ownership of the restaurant in 1969, continues the tradition of quality food and excellent service that has made Lamb's a dining institution.

John Speros succinctly describes Lamb's place in the community: "We don't try to compete with the elegant dining houses or prepare gourmet food. We try to give customers the very best meal we can at the most reasonable price." The formula works, for Lamb's serves 1000 to 1200 customers each day. What is more remarkable is that two-thirds of the customers are regulars who eat at Lamb's every weekday, one of the reasons for the large menu. "We feed the same people every day, so we have to offer a wide selection." Still, for many regulars, the menu replaces the calendar as daily specials announce the day of week—chicken pot pie and Wednesday are synonymous.

It is said that Lamb's is "where the elite meet to eat" lunch. A more accurate statement is that Lamb's clientele represents a cross-section of the downtown community—government officials and businessmen to students and working men—drawn by "honest food at honest prices." As Speros notes, "People don't come back day after day and pay good money for bad food." Whether one sits at the 21-seat counter, the longest in the state, or in the rear dining room featuring high-backed booths and linen-draped tables, Lamb's is truly a culinary "home-away-from-home" for Salt Lakers.

169 South Main   364-7166
Salt Lake City

SEAFOOD COCKTAIL

½ pound fresh halibut
½ pound fresh salmon
Juice of ½ lemon
Salt
1 bay leaf
1 rib celery, finely diced

1 green onion, finely chopped
White pepper to taste
½ head lettuce, shredded
6 lemon wedges
SEAFOOD COCKTAIL SAUCE

1. Poach the fish in water to cover with the lemon juice, a pinch of salt, and the bay leaf until the flesh is opaque and beginning to flake, 5 to 6 minutes. Drain and cool.
2. Coarsely shred or flake the fish. Gently combine with the celery and green onion. Add salt and white pepper to taste.
3. Serve on a bed of shredded lettuce with a lemon wedge. Top with SEAFOOD COCKTAIL SAUCE.

SEAFOOD COCKTAIL SAUCE

2 cups tomato ketchup
Juice of 1 lemon
1 teaspoon horseradish

1 teaspoon Worcestershire sauce
2-3 drops Tabasco sauce

Thoroughly combine all ingredients. Refrigerate at least 24 hours before using to allow flavors to meld.

LENTIL SOUP

10 ounces dried lentils	1 bay leaf
2 quarts BEEF STOCK or water	1 beef bouillon cube
1 cup salad oil	2 teaspoons salt
1 medium onion, chopped	½ teaspoon white pepper
1 cup chopped celery	1 cup flour
1 cup chopped carrots	1 cup tomato sauce
1 tablespoon garlic powder	2 quarts BEEF STOCK
1 tablespoon Greek oregano	5 tablespoons cider vinegar
1½ teaspoons paprika	Tomato paste as needed

1. Wash the lentils. Soak them overnight in water to cover. Drain.

2. Bring the lentils to a boil in 2 quarts of BEEF STOCK or water. Cook, uncovered, until tender, about 45 minutes. Expect to lose about half of the liquid.

3. Meanwhile, in another pot, combine the salad oil, onion, celery, carrots, garlic powder, oregano, paprika, bay leaf, bouillon cube, salt, and pepper. Sauté the vegetables until tender, 6 to 8 minutes. Add the flour and tomato sauce. Mix well and simmer at least 15 minutes, stirring occasionally. Add the 2 quarts of BEEF STOCK, and vinegar. Bring to a boil.

4. When the lentils are tender, add both lentils and their cooking liquid to the BEEF STOCK. Bring to a boil and simmer for at least 30 minutes. Add salt and pepper to taste. If desired, add 1 to 2 tablespoons of tomato paste for flavor and color.

BEEF STOCK

3 pounds beef bones	1 large onion, quartered
4 quarts cold water	1 large tomato, quartered
1 stalk celery with leaves, coarsely choppped	6 black peppercorns
	2 teaspoons salt
1 large carrot, coarsely chopped	1 bay leaf

1. Wash the beef bones. Place the bones in cold water and bring to a boil. Skim surface scum as necessary.

2. Add remaining ingredients and simmer 3 to 4 hours.

3. Strain, cool quickly, and refrigerate. Remove hardened fat. If the stock tastes too weak, boil to reduce further in order to concentrate the flavor.

We always keep a stock pot going and keep tossing in bones, onion skins, carrot and tomato peelings, celery leaves, and so on. At the end of the week, we strain out the vegetables. You can't duplicate that kind of stock at home. Actually, bouillon cubes, beef base, or canned broth works just fine in recipes where the stock is just background flavoring.

BRAISED LAMB SHANKS

6 (12-ounce) lamb shanks	2 medium onions, chopped
2 tablespoons paprika	3-4 cups BEEF STOCK
1 tablespoon garlic powder	1 (8-ounce) can tomato sauce
1 teaspoon allspice	1 (6-ounce) can tomato paste
Salt	2 tablespoons lemon juice
Fresh ground black pepper	Chopped parsley for garnish

1. Wash and dry the lamb shanks. Place in large pot or small roasting pan. Rub the paprika, garlic powder, and allspice into the meat. Sprinkle with the salt and pepper. Distribute the onions over the meat, pressing so that the onions adhere to the meat. Cover and refrigerate overnight.

2. Preheat the oven to 375°. Bake the lamb shanks without adding any liquid for about 2 hours, turning occasionally, until browned. Add 1 cup of the BEEF STOCK and bake 25 to 30 minutes more.

3. Remove from the oven and place on the stove over medium heat. Add additional BEEF STOCK to just cover the lamb shanks. Remove the lamb shanks. Skim most of the grease from the broth. Stir in the tomato sauce, tomato paste, and lemon juice. Add salt, pepper, and garlic powder to taste. Return the lamb shanks to the sauce, reduce the heat to medium low, and simmer until the meat is tender, about 2 hours.

continued...

4. Remove the lamb shanks to a serving platter. Skim the grease from the sauce and spoon the sauce over the shanks. Garnish with chopped parsley.

If the sauce seems too thick, thin with additional BEEF STOCK. If the sauce seems too thin, thicken with flour or cornstarch dissolved in water.

RICE PILAF

⅓ cup lemon juice	2 cups long grain rice, washed
4 tablespoons butter	3¾ cups chicken broth
1 teaspoon salt	Black pepper to taste

1. In a saucepan bring the lemon juice, butter, and salt to a boil. Add the rice and cook, stirring frequently, until the liquid is absorbed by the rice.
2. Meanwhile, in another saucepan, bring the chicken broth to a boil. Add the boiling broth to the rice, cover, and simmer over low heat until all liquid has been absorbed and the rice is tender, about 20 minutes. Add pepper and more butter to taste.

FRENCH FRIED ZUCCHINI

2 medium zucchini	1 egg
2 cups milk	½ cup flour (approximately)

1. Wash the zucchini and cut into ¼-inch thick slices.
2. Beat the milk and eggs together. Dip the zucchini slices into the milk and egg wash, coat lightly with flour, and deep fry until golden brown, 3 to 4 minutes. Serve immediately.

RICE PUDDING

1 *cup long grain white rice*	4 *eggs*
8 *cups plus 2 cups whole milk*	2 *teaspoons vanilla*
1 *cup plus ¼ cup sugar*	*Ground cinnamon to taste*

1. Wash and drain the rice. Combine the rice, 8 cups of milk, and 1 cup of sugar in a large saucepan. Cook over medium heat, stirring occasionally, until the rice is tender, about 25 minutes.

2. In a mixing bowl, combine the eggs, 2 cups milk, ¼ cup sugar, and vanilla. Beat well to blend ingredients thoroughly.

3. When the rice is tender, add the egg mixture and cook over medium heat until the liquid just begins to boil. Remove from the heat and let cool. Refrigerate until cold. Serve topped with ground cinnamon.

For variation, add raisins or the grated rind of an orange or lemon.

Le Parisien

Dinner for Four

Champignons à la Grecque

Ris de Veau Forestiere

Salade Verte

Chateaubriand

Pommes Dauphine

Carottes Glacées

Crème Caramel

Wines:

With the Sweetbreads—Chateau Martinet, Saint Emilion, 1979

With the Chateaubriand—Laboure-Roi, Pommard, 1981

Max Mercier, Owner-Executive Chef

LE PARISIEN

Since 1970 the chef's toque atop a flowing mustache has symbolized the expert food preparation and dining pleasure at Max Mercier's Le Parisien. When Mercier, who was born near Bordeaux, decided to open his own restaurant in Salt Lake City, his immediate concerns were financial instead of culinary. "Although I was trained in fine French restaurants, I didn't have the money to provide that kind of decor, so I used burlap instead of velvet on the walls, barnwood instead of oak, and made my own booths and tables." The result was an informal, charming restaurant in the mode of a French "auberge" and an Italian "trattoria."

He then created a cuisine as straightforward and traditional as the decor. Fresh seafood specials are posted daily, but regulars return repeatedly to such menu staples as boeuf bourguignon, onion soup gratinée, and lasagna. "Authentic, basic food, not extravagent but always made from the freshest and best quality products available on the market" is how Mercier describes his cuisine. His salad dressings, a classic vinaigrette and a new papaya chutney, are sold in specialty shops and supermarkets throughout the Intermountain West.

The comfortable atmosphere adds to the popularity of Le Parisien. Rotating exhibits of the work of local artists adorn the walls, providing a touch of intimacy and personality; so do the high-backed booths, which provide coziness and privacy without a feeling of confinement. "No one feels out of place in my restaurant whether in sneakers or on the way to the theatre," notes Mercier. "The entire staff does whatever is necessary to meet the needs of the customer. Our motto is good food, good service, and a pleasant atmosphere at a reasonable price." A member of the Chaine des Rotisseurs, the World Cooks and Chefs Society, and the American Culinary Federation, "Max," as he is familiarly known, served for three years as president of the Beehive Chefs Association and was named Chef of the Year for 1983-84.

417 South 300 East   364-5223
Salt Lake City

CHAMPIGNONS À LA GRECQUE

1 *pound small button mushrooms,*
   cleaned but not stemmed
¼ *cup white wine*
½ *teaspoon black peppercorns*
¼ *teaspoon thyme*

1 *teaspoon salt*
2 *bay leaves*
½ *teaspoon Tabasco sauce*
2 *tablespoons olive oil*

1. In a ceramic or glass bowl, combine the mushrooms with the wine, peppercorns, thyme, salt, bay leaves, and Tabasco. Set aside.

2. Preheat a medium skillet over high heat until very hot. Add the olive oil. When the oil is very hot, quickly pour into the skillet the mushrooms and marinade. Cover immediately to preserve vapors and cook, tossing occasionally, for 3 minutes or until the mushrooms are tender but still slightly firm. Remove from the heat and let cool. Rinse the skillet with a little water and pour over the mushrooms.

3. Serve the mushrooms at room temperature on a lettuce leaf.

Mushrooms must be cooked quickly. They are 90 percent water, so if they are cooked too long, the water is lost and all that remains is a gummy, tough mass.

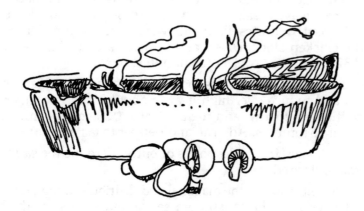

RIS DE VEAU FORESTIERE

1 pound sweetbreads
1 cup white vinegar
4 cups water
5 tablespoons butter
1 carrot, finely diced
1 stalk celery, finely diced
1 medium onion, finely diced
10 black peppercorns
2 sprigs parsley, stems included, finely chopped
2 bay leaves
1 teaspoon salt
½ teaspoon thyme
3 cups chicken stock (see index)

2 shallots, finely chopped
½ cup Madeira wine
1 cup BROWN SAUCE
¼ cup sliced white mushrooms
½ ounce dried morels, soaked in milk to cover, until plumped
¼ cup sliced chanterelles or other field mushrooms
Salt or fresh ground black pepper to taste
1 tablespoon heavy (whipping) cream (optional)
Chopped parsley for garnish

1. Soak the sweetbreads with the vinegar in cold water to cover for 4 hours. Drain. Transfer the sweetbreads to a pot of cold water. Bring to a boil over high heat and blanch for 5 minutes. Transfer the sweetbreads to a bowl of cold water to cool. When cool, remove the filaments or membranes, breaking the sweetbreads into sections if necessary. Reserve.

2. Melt 2 tablespoons of the butter in a medium pot. Make a *mirepoix* by sautéing the carrots, celery, and onion along with the peppercorns, parsley, bay leaves, salt, and thyme until the vegetables begin to "sweat," about 3 minutes. Place the sweetbreads on top of the *mirepoix*. Add the chicken stock, cover, and bring to a boil. Transfer to a pre-heated 375° oven and cook for 50 minutes.

3. Sauté the shallots in 1 tablespoon of butter until golden. Add the Madeira and reduce over high heat to about 2 tablespoons of liquid. Reduce the heat to low, add the BROWN SAUCE and mushrooms, and simmer for 15 minutes. Add salt and pepper to taste.

4. Off the heat, swirl in 2 tablespoons of butter to refine the sauce. Stir in the cream if desired.

5. Slice the sweetbreads on the diagonal and distribute among four serving plates. Cover with the mushroom sauce and garnish with chopped parsley.

It is important to reduce the Madeira over high heat so as to burn off the alcohol. To drink alcohol in the form of wine is one thing, but to eat it is quite another. The alcohol in wine when combined with food will often cause heartburn or indigestion unless burned off.

The dried morels must be washed and rinsed thoroughly because they are full of sand.

If BROWN SAUCE is not available, substitute 1 cup of the broth in which the sweetbreads were cooked. Add Kitchen Bouquet for color.

BROWN SAUCE

Brown sauce, Fond de Veau Lie, is the base for all brown sauces used in French cooking. It is nothing more than concentrated or thickened Brown Veal Stock (see index). There are four ways to make the 1 cup of brown sauce needed for this recipe. First, whisk into 1 cup of boiling Brown Veal Stock 1½ tablespoons of cooked roux. Second, whisk into the boiling stock 1½ tablespoons of flour mixed with water or stock to the consistency of a paste. Third, whisk into the boiling stock 1½ tablespoons of flour creamed with an equal amount of butter (beurre manié). Fourth, whisk in 1½ tablespoons of flour. In the first three methods liquid, butter or water, will help distribute the flour evenly; in the fourth method, vigorous whisking is required. The amount of thickening will vary, so it is best to use less than the full amount of thickening and add more if necessary. This brown sauce should be thin but not runny.

SALADE VERT

1 head Boston lettuce
1 head red leaf lettuce
8 tomato wedges

8 black olives
   PAPAYA CHUTNEY DRESSING

Wash and dry the lettuce. Tear the lettuce into bite-size pieces and distribute among four chilled salad plates. Garnish each salad with 2 tomato wedges and 2 black olives. Top with PAPAYA CHUTNEY DRESSING.

PAPAYA CHUTNEY DRESSING

5 tablespoons mayonnaise
5 tablespoons salad (corn) oil
2 tablespoons papaya chutney
1 tablespoon cider vinegar
2-3 drops lemon juice

Dash of Tabasco sauce
Dash of Worcestershire sauce
Dash of A-1 sauce
Pinch of sugar
Pinch of salt
Pinch of pepper

Combine all ingredients in a bowl. Beat with a wire whisk for 2 minutes so that the ingredients are mixed thoroughly. Adjust seasonings.

Salad dressings are very personal. You have to keep adjusting seasonings until it is just right for your taste.

CHATEAUBRIAND

2 *(1-pound each) beef*
tenderloin heads
Salt and pepper

Oil
2 *tablespoons brandy (optional)*
BÉARNAISE SAUCE

1. Sprinkle the tenderloin heads with salt and pepper. Rub with oil. Sear the tenderloin in a preheated skillet over high heat, 3 minutes on each side or a total of 6 minutes. Place the skillet in a preheated 375° oven and finish to desired doneness, 10 minutes for medium.

2. At the moment of serving, pour warmed brandy into the skillet and ignite. When the flame dies out, remove the tenderloin from the skillet. Cut each tenderloin head against the grain into 8 slices. Serve 4 slices per person accompanied by BÉARNAISE SAUCE.

Specifically ask the butcher for tenderloin heads. Each section of the tenderloin is used for a different dish. The "head" or largest end of the tenderloin is used for chateaubriand, the middle section is used for tournedos, the smaller end is used for filet mignon, and the tail is used for brochettes.

The flambé is for show. It is not traditional when serving Chateaubriand, but our customers like it. It is an optional treatment.

BÉARNAISE SAUCE is an accompaniment to meat. It should never be spooned over the meat, but instead passed in a gravy boat or spooned at the side of the meat like a chutney or horseradish.

BÉARNAISE SAUCE

3 egg yolks
1 tablespoon water
½ pound butter, melted and
  kept warm

1 shallot, finely chopped
½ cup red wine vinegar
1 teaspoon tarragon
  Pinch of black pepper
  Salt

1. Place the egg yolks and water in a stainless steel mixing bowl over a double boiler of simmering water. Beat vigorously with a wire whisk, using a *Figure 8* motion, until the yolks first become light and fluffy and then hold a thick ribbon when the whisk is lifted. Add the warm, melted butter in a thin stream, whisking constantly. Do not add the milky sediment at the bottom of the butter. Keep warm.

2. Place the chopped shallot, vinegar, tarragon, and pepper in a small saucepan. Bring to a boil over medium high heat and cook until it reduces to a very moist but solid mass.

3. Whisk the shallot reduction into the egg and butter sauce base. Season with salt and pepper to taste. Keep warm until serving time.

Béarnaise Sauce must be kept warm until ready to use because it cannot be reheated. We suggest putting it into a stainless steel mixing bowl, covering with plastic wrap, and setting the bowl over a double boiler or pot of hot water. This is done off the flame or the eggs will cook and the butter will separate.

An egg and butter sauce will split; that is, the butter will separate if it becomes too hot or too cold. If the sauce splits because it is too hot, put 1 tablespoon of cold water in a mixing bowl and slowly add the sauce, whisking constantly. If the sauce splits because it is too cold, rewarm the sauce over a double boiler to lukewarm. Put 1 tablespoon of hot water in a bowl and slowly add the sauce, whisking constantly.

Adding the melted butter to the eggs is a simple yet tricky step. The butter must be warm, approximately the same temperature as the eggs, or the sauce will split. Do not add the milky sediment at the bottom of a container of melted butter. It contains unwanted milk solids and water that can mar the sauce.

Béarnaise sauce is a strongly flavored sauce that is an excellent accompaniment to strongly flavored meats. It really depends less on the kind of meat than the method of preparation. For example, poached salmon demands a light sauce such as Hollandaise but grilled salmon can stand up to a Béarnaise. The basic rule is that delicately flavored meats require light sauces, strongly flavored meats demand powerful sauces.

POMMES DAUPHINE

6 ounces mashed potatoes	White pepper
6 ounces pâte à choux (see index)	Fresh ground nutmeg
Salt	Oil for deep frying

1. Thoroughly combine the mashed potatoes and pâte à choux. Season with the salt, white pepper, and nutmeg to taste.

2. Heat the oil to deep frying temperature. Drop walnut-size pieces of dough, 4 or 5 at a time, into the oil and fry until golden brown. Drain on paper toweling and repeat with remaining dough.

For best results, use dry mashed potatoes. That is, simply mash cooked potatoes without adding butter or milk or seasoning.

CAROTTES GLACÉES

½ pound carrots   1 teaspoon sugar
2 tablespoons butter   Salt

1. Peel the carrots and slice on the diagonal in ⅛-inch thick pieces. Blanch in boiling water until just tender, 8 to 10 minutes. Drain.

2. Melt the butter over medium high heat in a skillet. Add the carrot slices. Sprinkle with the sugar and a pinch of salt. Sauté until the sugar granules have dissolved and the carrots are warmed through and covered with a glaze.

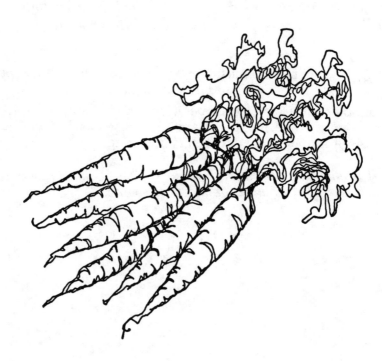

CRÈME CARAMEL

⅓ cup plus ¼ cup sugar, divided
3 tablespoons water
½ cup plus 2 tablespoons milk
½ cup heavy (whipping) cream

¾ teaspoon vanilla extract
1 teaspoon grated lemon rind
1 whole egg
5 egg yolks

1. Cook ⅓ cup sugar and the water in a saucepan over medium high heat until the sugar-water begins to thicken, bubble, and turn brown. Immediately pour the caramelized sugar into 4 ramekin, custard, or individual soufflé cups, turning quickly to coat the bottom and sides of the cups. Set aside.

2. In a saucepan, scald the milk and cream. Cool.

3. Using an electric mixer or wire whisk, beat the ¼ cup sugar, vanilla, lemon rind, egg, and yolks until well blended and fluffy.

4. Pour the milk mixture into the egg mixture, whisking vigorously until thoroughly blended. Strain the custard.

5. Divide the custard among the caramel coated cups. Place the filled cups in a bain marie (water bath) of cool water. The water level should reach half way up the sides of the cups. Place in a preheated 350° oven until the custard sets, 25 to 35 minutes. Let cool. Refrigerate until serving time.

6. To serve, unmold onto individual dessert plates.

To unmold the custard, run the sharp point of a knife between the edge of the custard and the cup at a depth of no more than ¼-inch. Invert the cup over the serving plate. Raise the cup 1 to 2 inches off the plate at an angle (to allow air penetration) and shake vigorously until the custard falls on the plate.

The sides of the custard should be smooth. If there are "bubbles" around the edge of the custard, the oven became too hot thus causing the water to boil and "cook" the custard. Check periodically to see that the water bath is hot but not boiling.

Liaison

Dinner for Four

Compound Potato-Leek Soup

Green Salad with Piquant Vinaigrette

Grapefruit Ice

Chicken Breasts with Three-Grape and Three-Wine Sauce

Mixed Greens Sauté

Yam-Squash Julienne

Fruit and Cheese, Cookies and Nuts

Wine:

With the Chicken—Kenwood Chardonnay, 1981

With the Dessert—Sandeman Vintage Port, 1966

Arthur H. "Bub" Horne, Owner-Chef

Liaison, a small, intimate, impeccably appointed restaurant, is the unmistakable expression of the personality of owner-chef Arthur H. "Bub" Horne. Horne, who cooked in several prominent New York City restaurants after graduating from the Culinary Institute of America in 1976, opened Liaison in 1982 with a specific objective in mind. "The theme of this restaurant is serious food. I'm not here to get rich, to have a dining room full of fancy artwork and antiques, or to redecorate four times a year. We're dedicated to preparing quality food as freshly and as appropriately as possible. We don't cut corners or rely on food that is frozen, prepackaged, produced by machines, or laden with chemicals. Someday I'd like Liaison to be a world class restaurant."

Despite the name, Liaison is not a French restaurant. Horne is emphatic: "This is an American restaurant—there is nothing French here except some basic culinary techniques." The name was chosen because the chemical definition of the term—a coming together of two or more units in a cohesive force or group—also defines Horne's culinary philosophy. "Because America has no real indigenous tradition of fine cuisine but instead is made up of the cooking of many nationalities, I freely borrow the concepts and techniques of all cultures in preparing American products." An example is his excellent Veal Stir Fry, which blends American ingredients with Asian techniques.

While the entire eclectic menu changes seasonally, much of the menu, from appetizers through desserts, changes daily. Sometimes the menu changes during the course of the evening, and it is not unusual for each member of a dinner party to receive a different starch or vegetable. "Food for the moment. That's our creed. We take the freshest ingredients available and prepare food on a command performance basis. Except for soups, desserts, and certain sauces, the food is prepared for each individual when ordered. But our goal is consistency—food that is consistently good, not consistently the same."

1352 South 2100 East   583-8144
Salt Lake City

COMPOUND POTATO-LEEK SOUP

2 tablespoons butter
1 large leek, white and yellow parts only, chopped
1 stalk celery, leaves removed and chopped
½ green bell pepper, chopped
½ teaspoon thyme
½ teaspoon nutmeg
½ teaspoon white pepper

½ teaspoon cayenne pepper
1 large bay leaf
3 tablespoons flour
1 quart CHICKEN STOCK, simmering
4 medium white potatoes, chopped
SPINACH-WATERCRESS PURÉE
RED BEET PURÉE
½ cup heavy (whipping) cream

1. Melt the butter in a pot over moderate heat and sauté the leeks, celery, green pepper, and the spices until the leeks are limp. To avoid discoloring the white soup, do not use an aluminum pot and take care not to brown the leeks.

2. Add the flour and cook for 4 to 5 minutes over low heat, stirring frequently, until the flour is cooked and fully incorporated into the vegetable mixture. Do not let the flour brown.

3. Slowly add ½ to 1 cup of the simmering CHICKEN STOCK to the vegetable-flour mixture. Stir well.

4. When the mixture is smooth, add the remainder of the stock and the potatoes. Cook, covered, over moderate heat until the potatoes are very well done, about 25 minutes.

5. When the potatoes are done, strain the vegetables. Reserve the broth. Purée the vegetables to a fine consistency in a food processor or food mill. Pass the purée through a medium strainer. Add the reserved broth to make a smooth soup of desired consistency. Chill the soup and any remaining broth in the refrigerator until cold, at least 3 to 4 hours.

6. Make SPINACH-WATERCRESS PURÉE. Chill.

7. Make RED BEET PURÉE. Chill.

continued…

8. Construct the compound soup just prior to serving. Slowly stir the heavy cream into the white potato-leek soup. Add additional reserved broth or cream if the soup seems too thick, but remember that the soup must have a fairly dense consistency to support the purées. Ladle about ¾ cup of soup into large, shallow, chilled soup bowls. Add 2 to 3 tablespoons each of the SPINACH-WATERCRESS and RED BEET purées in a visually appealing design.

Baking potatoes contain too much starch, red potatoes insufficient starch, to be used in this recipe. If leeks are unavailable, use a medium yellow onion, chopped and parboiled 10 to 15 seconds in boiling water to remove the sulfur. Heating the dried spices and herbs in butter will improve their taste because the active "flavors" are largely oil soluble.

Use your imagination in constructing an interesting design for the soup. You can form circles of various sizes with the purées. You can use the green purée to form a line bisecting the white soup and make a contrasting circle with the red purée. Be creative! You might even pass the purées separately and let each person be a culinary artist!

CHICKEN STOCK

2 chicken carcasses or about 5 pounds chicken bones	1 tablespoon fresh ginger, chopped (optional)
1 onion, coarsely chopped	1 star anise (optional)
1 carrot, coarsely chopped	1 teaspoon thyme (optional)
1 celery stalk, coarsely chopped	1 bay leaf (optional)
2 cloves garlic, coarsely chopped	Salt

1. Wash the chicken bones in cold water. Bring to a boil in heavily salted water to cover. When the water reaches a boil, immediately drain the bones and rinse again in cold water.

2. For Chinese-style stock, place the bones in a stock pot with the onion, carrot, celery, garlic, ginger, star anise, and enough water to cover the bones by 1 inch. Cook at a strong boil for 1 hour.

3. For French-style chicken broth, place the bones in a stock pot with enough water to cover by 1 inch. Bring to a boil, reduce heat, and simmer slowly for 5 to 6 hours. Add the onion, carrot, celery, 1 clove of garlic, thyme and bay leaf. Simmer for 30 minutes.

4. When the stock is cooked, strain, discard solids, and chill. Degrease before using. Chicken stock will keep in the refrigerator for 2 to 3 days. If the stock is to be kept longer, every 3 days bring to a boil for 5 minutes and rechill. Stock freezes well for several months.

The difference between stock and broth is that stock is made from bones while broth is made from bones and meat. Wing and leg bones make the best stock. When cooking stock, it is important that the bones are always covered with water because exposed bones quickly deteriorate and can turn sour. Add hot water to the stock if necessary to keep the bones covered. It is important to chill cooked stock quickly because bacteria also love chicken soup. If the cooked stock seems to lack flavor, reduce further by boiling to concentrate the flavor.

SPINACH-WATERCRESS PURÉE

1 teaspoon salt	½ green bell pepper, chopped
8 ounces fresh spinach	½ teaspoon dried tarragon,
6 ounces fresh watercress	or fresh if available
1 ounce fresh parsley, stems only	½ teaspoon dried basil,
(the leaves turn bitter	or fresh if available
when cooked)	½ cup chilled POTATO-LEEK SOUP
1 medium scallion, green and	1 teaspoon Pernod, or to taste
white parts chopped	

1. In a saucepan bring to boil enough water to cover the greens.

2. When the water reaches a full boil, add the salt, greens, scallion, pepper, and herbs. Cook, uncovered, until the greens are tender, about 4 to 5 minutes.

continued...

3. When tender, remove from heat and immediately plunge into cold water to set the bright green color. When the greens are cold, drain well and then gently squeeze to remove excess water.

4. Purée the greens in a food processor or blender, adding approximately ½ cup of the chilled POTATO-LEEK SOUP to make a smooth purée. Strain, add the Pernod, mix well, and chill in the refrigerator until serving time.
   Greens will lose color if added to water before it reaches a boil or if cooked in a covered pot.

RED BEET PURÉE

4 small red beets, trimmed but unpeeled	¼ cup chilled POTATO-LEEK SOUP
1 teaspoon vinegar	1 teaspoon Kümmel
	Salt and pepper to taste

1. In a small saucepan cook the beets in enough water to cover and the vinegar until very tender, 30 to 35 minutes. Plunge the cooked beets into cold water. When cool enough to handle, remove the skins.

2. Purée the beets in a food processor or blender, adding approximately ¼ cup of the chilled POTATO-LEEK SOUP to make a smooth purée. Add the Kümmel, salt and pepper to taste, and chill in the refrigerator until serving time.

GREEN SALAD WITH PIQUANT VINAIGRETTE

½ head Bibb lettuce
½ head red leaf lettuce
2 medium tomatoes

1 large carrot
PIQUANT VINAIGRETTE

1. Wash and dry the lettuce, then tear into bite-size pieces.
2. Seed the tomatoes and cut into julienne strips.
3. Peel and grate the carrot.
4. Arrange the lettuce, tomato, and carrot on individual chilled salad plates and serve with PIQUANT VINAIGRETTE.

PIQUANT VINAIGRETTE

2 large cloves garlic
4 ounces fresh basil leaves
Salt to taste

⅓ cup olive oil
1½ cups red wine vinegar
1½ cups water

1. In a blender process the garlic, basil, a pinch of salt, and enough water to make a smooth pesto (paste).
2. Combine the basil pesto, oil, vinegar, and 1½ cups water. Whisk, blend, or shake until all ingredients are well incorporated. Add salt to taste. Serve immediately.

GRAPEFRUIT ICE

1 cup sugar
½ cup water
1 quart pink grapefruit juice,
    room temperature
4 grapefruit sections,
    membranes removed

8 fresh juniper berries,
    washed and lightly bruised
Mint leaves
⅓ cup gin fragrant of juniper,
    (e.g. Gordon's)

1. Over medium heat dissolve the sugar in the water; heat to the soft thread stage (216-220°). Slowly pour the syrup into the tepid grapefruit juice, stirring constantly until well blended. Add additional sugar if the mixture is too tart. Chill.

2. Process in an ice cream maker according to manufacturer's instructions. Store in the freezer for at least 3 hours but not longer than 6.

3. Garnish each serving of the ice with 1 grapefruit segment, 2 fresh juniper berries, and/or a mint leaf. Sprinkle with gin to taste.

Either fresh or canned grapefruit juice may be used. If using fresh juice, seed but do not strain the pulp; if using canned juice, buy the best available product as the taste of the ice depends on the quality of the juice. The grapefruit juice must be room temperature or slightly warmer to prevent the syrup from crystallizing. When adding sugar to taste, it should be remembered that foods taste less sweet when cold than when at warmer temperatures.

CHICKEN BREASTS WITH
THREE-GRAPE AND THREE-WINE SAUCE

12 green grapes
12 Pink Riesling grapes
12 Pinot Noir grapes
 4 whole chicken breasts,
    boned and closely trimmed
 1 cup flour seasoned with salt
    and pepper to taste

Oil for sautéing
 1 cup Chablis or other white wine
½ cup vermouth or a
    sparkling wine
 1 cup heavy (whipping) cream
½ cup sherry, preferably a fino
    such as Tio Pepe

1. Halve the grapes; seed if necessary. Reserve.

2. Lightly flour the chicken breasts on skin side only with the seasoned flour.

3. Heat the oil in a large, heavy pan over medium heat. When the oil is hot, sauté the chicken breasts, skin side down, until the skin is nicely browned and most of the flesh has become opaque, about 6 minutes. Do not turn the breasts while cooking. Remove to a heated platter.

4. Pour off the oil from the pan and pat dry with a paper towel. Return the pan to high heat and deglaze with the Chablis and vermouth, scraping up any browned bits. Continue boiling until the wines are reduced to a thick syrup.

5. Lower heat to medium. Add the cream and grapes. Whisk until the cream sauce is reduced and thickened. Add the sherry and quickly whisk to incorporate with the sauce.

6. To serve, place one chicken breast on a warmed dinner plate, top with grape and wine sauce, and accompany with MIXED GREENS SAUTÉ and YAM-SQUASH JULIENNE.

Any three grape varieties of different size, color, and taste can be used, and any two complimentary white wines can be used with the sherry.

MIXED GREENS SAUTÉ

3 ounces Napa cabbage, shredded
3 ounces mustard greens,
    shredded

3 ounces ruby chard, shredded
2 tablespoons butter
1 teaspoon lemon juice
   Salt and pepper

1. Clean the greens thoroughly by soaking and rinsing twice. Par boil in rapidly boiling water 15 to 20 seconds to soften and to remove any petrol base insecticides. Drain.

2. Melt the butter in a medium size sauté pan. Add the lemon juice and greens. Sprinkle with salt and pepper and sauté briefly until tender. Adjust seasonings to taste.

My mother says this is the best vegetable we serve at Liaison. It is magnificent!

YAM-SQUASH JULIENNE

7 ounces butternut squash
7 ounces sweet yams
1 tablespoon butter

½ tablespoon fresh dill,
    finely chopped
   Salt and pepper
1 teaspoon vermouth

1. Peel the squash and yams and cut into julienne strips. Blanch the strips in boiling, salted water for 30 seconds. Drain well.

2. Melt the butter in a medium size sauté pan. Add the warm vegetables and sauté briefly with the dill and a sprinkling of salt and pepper. When the vegetables approach the desired doneness, finish with vermouth flambé, stirring rapidly to distribute the wine.

Our customers tell us these are the best carrots they have ever eaten. Sometimes we tell them what they have eaten.

FRUIT and CHEESE, COOKIES and NUTS

12 *walnut or pecan halves*
Butter for sautéing
Salt to taste

4 *slices Brie cheese*
Assorted fresh berries
4 *spice cookies*
8 *CHOCOLATE DUCATS*

1. Briefly sauté the walnut or pecan halves in butter. Salt to taste.

2. Arrange the cheese, fruits, nuts, and cookies on a dessert plate and serve with a vintage port.

CHOCOLATE DUCATS

3 *ounces semi-sweet chocolate*
8 *tablespoons butter,*
at room temperature
¾ *cup sugar*
½ *cup cocoa powder*
1 *egg, lightly beaten*

2 *tablespoons orange zest,*
finely chopped
1 *tablespoon orange liqueur*
10 *ounces plain butter or*
short bread cookies
(Lorna Doone recommended),
coarsely crushed

1. Melt the chocolate and butter over low heat. Add the remaining ingredients except the cookies and mix well. Gently incorporate the cookies. Refrigerate until the chocolate mixture hardens sufficiently to work by hand.

2. Place the chocolate mixture on waxed paper and roll by hand into a small cylinder 1- to 1½-inches in diameter. Be sure to roll the cylinder tightly or the cookies will crumble when cut. Refrigerate.

3. Just prior to serving, cut the cylinder into ⅜-inch circles (ducats).

Dinner for Four

Baked Oysters Lafitte

Coco Beer Shrimp

Seafood Filé Gumbo

Crawfish and Veal Etouffée

Jambalaya Rice

Hush Puppies

Creole Bread Pudding with Whiskey Sauce

Wines:

With the Appetizers—Joseph Phelps Sauvignon Blanc, 1982

With the Crawfish and Veal—Fisher Chardonnay, 1981
or
BV Latoure Cabernet Sauvignon, 1976

Dr. Owen and Barbara Reese, Owners

NEW ORLEANS CAFE

The New Orleans Cafe opened in March, 1982, as a tiny storefront cafe with seating for 35 patrons. An instant hit, The New Orleans within the year moved to its present location in the historic Crane Building and became a 100-seat, full-service Creole and Cajun restaurant. Dr. Owen Reese, a wine expert, has assembled an impressive collection of special vintages to complement the distinctive cuisine. His wife, Barbara, a talented cook and hostess, oversees the menu, service, and decor.

The dramatic black-and-white dining room, Mardi Gras posters, and neon "fish" and "crustaceans" promise patrons both good food and good fun. The good times do roll at the New Orleans, especially on Thursday, Friday and Saturday nights and during the special Sunday Brunch when the Salt Lake Good Times Band is on hand to play foot-stomping Dixieland jazz favorites. The food, the music, the atmosphere, and the copies of the New Orleans *Times Picayune* combine to transport diners to Bayou country.

The Reeses are committed to offering authentic regional cuisine. Classic Louisiana specialties fill the menu—Roast Cajun Duck and Blackened Redfish, Froglegs and Jambalaya, Chicken Rochambeau and Crab Biscay, Red Beans and Rice and Pecan Pie. Regulars know to watch the blackboards for daily postings of fresh seafood specialties. The Reeses promise customers who sample the "classic Cajun specialities" that they will "never go back to eating just 'food' again." Creole and Cajun food, the lone indigenous American cuisine, and jazz, the unique American contribution to music—an unbeatable combination.

307 West 200 South   363-6573
Salt Lake City

BAKED OYSTERS LAFITTE

16 *fresh oysters*
2 *tablespoons butter*
2 *shallots, finely chopped*
1 *clove garlic, finely chopped*
¼ *cup white wine*
2 *cups heavy (whipping) cream*
½ *teaspoon white pepper*

Salt to taste
2 *sprigs fresh dill*
1 *tablespoon grated Parmesan cheese*
8 *ounces crab meat, shredded*
Grated Parmesan cheese, as needed
Minced parsley for garnish

1. Clean and shuck oysters, leaving meat on a half-shell. Shuck the oysters over a bowl in order to reserve as much of the juice as possible. Set aside.

2. In a skillet over medium heat, melt the butter. Sauté the shallots and garlic until soft and translucent. Add the wine and reduce to a thick syrup. Add the cream and reserved oyster juice. Reduce until the cream is slightly thickened. Add the white pepper and salt to taste. Add the dill and cheese. Blend well and remove from the heat.

3. Arrange the oysters on the half-shell on a baking sheet. Top with the shredded crab meat. Top with 1 to 2 teaspoons of the cream sauce. Sprinkle with grated Parmesan cheese to taste. Bake in 375° oven until the sauce is bubbling and the cheese has begun to brown. Sprinkle oysters with minced parsley and serve.

It is difficult to distinguish clearly between Cajun and Creole cooking. They are both traditional Louisiana cooking. The primary origin is French, but there are Spanish, Italian, African, and Native American influences as well. Generally speaking, Cajun is spicy, earthy, country cooking while Creole is more subtle urban cuisine. The appetizers and dessert in this menu are Creole, while the main dishes are Cajun.

COCO BEER SHRIMP

16 *large shrimp or prawns*   *Oil for deep frying*
   Flour   *PIQUANTE SAUCE*
   BEER BATTER   *APRICOT SAUCE*
 1 *pound grated or flaked coconut*

Shell and devein the shrimp, but leave the tails attached. Dust the shrimp lightly with flour and dip into the BEER BATTER to coat evenly. Allow excess batter to drip off, and then roll the shrimp in the coconut to coat generously. Deep fry at 350° until golden brown, 2 to 3 minutes. As an appetizer, serve 4 shrimp per person accompanied by PIQUANTE SAUCE and APRICOT SAUCE.

BEER BATTER

12 *ounces beer*   ½ *teaspoon cayenne pepper*
 1 *cup water*   ½ *teaspoon black pepper*
1½ *cups flour*   ½ *teaspoon white pepper*
 1 *egg*   1 *teaspoon salt*
                            Pinch of garlic powder

Thoroughly mix all ingredients in a large mixing bowl.

PIQUANTE SAUCE

2 cups ketchup
½ cup finely diced onion
¼ cup finely diced green
    bell pepper
¼ cup finely diced celery
½ teaspoon finely diced jalapeño
    pepper

1½ teaspoons black pepper
1½ teaspoons garlic powder
2 dashes Tabasco sauce
1 teaspoon Worcestershire sauce
½ teaspoon thyme
½ teaspoon salt

Thoroughly blend all ingredients several hours before using to allow flavors to meld.

APRICOT SAUCE

1 cup apricot jelly
1 cup fish stock (see index)
1 slice ginger (size and thickness
    of a quarter), finely shredded

1 bay leaf
Pinch of white pepper
Pinch of salt
Pinch of garlic powder

Mix all ingredients in a saucepan. Cook over low heat for 20 minutes, stirring occasionally.

SEAFOOD FILÉ GUMBO

¾ cup margarine (not butter)
2 cups chopped green bell pepper
2 cups chopped celery
2 cups chopped onion
1 clove garlic, minced
1 jalapeño pepper, diced
1 teaspoon salt
1 teaspoon white pepper
1 teaspoon ground black pepper
1 teaspoon dried thyme
1 teaspoon fresh thyme
1 teaspoon dried oregano

1 teaspoon fresh oregano
3 tablepoons filé powder
3 bay leaves
2 teaspoons paprika
5 cups SEAFOOD STOCK
1 teaspoon cayenne pepper or to taste
Tabasco sauce to taste
12 small oysters
½ pound bay shrimp
½ pound crab meat
½ pound white fish (cod or halibut), in bite-size pieces

1. Melt the margarine in a small soup pot. Add the bell peppers, celery, and onion. Sauté over medium heat for 5 minutes. Add the garlic, jalapeño, seasonings, and spices. Cook for 5 minutes, stirring constantly. Be sure to scrape the bottom of the pan as the mixture will tend to stick. The thick scrapings from the pan bottom add to the texture and flavor of the gumbo. Add the SEAFOOD STOCK and bring to a boil. Reduce the heat and simmer for 45 minutes. Add the cayenne pepper and Tabasco sauce to taste, about 1 teaspoon of cayenne and 2 dashes of Tabasco.

2. Just before serving, add the oysters, shrimp, crab, and white fish. Cover the pot, turn off the heat, and poach the seafood for 10 minutes.

Margarine, with its greater capacity to conduct heat and larger oil content, works much better than butter in developing the flavor, color, and texture of filé gumbo; however, the oil will separate during cooking and should be skimmed from the surface of the gumbo before adding the seafood.

Fresh and dried herbs have distinctly different tastes. We find the combination of fresh and dried herbs often provides just the right taste.

Filé powder, ground sassafras leaves normally mixed with ground bay leaf, is an essential ingredient in Cajun gumbos. It is available in most quality supermarkets.

This is a rather spicy dish. Many people are not accustomed to the fiery nature of Cajun cooking, so it is safer to add the heat at the end and adjust to taste. Gumbos are traditionally served over rice, with the blandness of the rice balancing the spiciness of the gumbo.

SEAFOOD STOCK

8 cups cold water	1 rib celery, coarsely chopped
1 medium onion, quartered	1 clove garlic, halved
	1½-2 pounds seafood trimmings

Add all ingredients to a pot. Bring to a boil, reduce heat, and simmer 4 to 8 hours adding additional water to keep trimmings covered. Strain. Seafood stock can be refrigerated 2 to 3 days or frozen for several months.

Any variety or combination of seafood trimmings can be used to make the stock—fish bones, crab shells, crawfish heads and claws, shrimp heads and shells. But never use fish skin, and never let the stock boil while cooking as it will become bitter.

CRAWFISH AND VEAL ETOUFFÉE

¼ pound margarine
1 cup diced green bell pepper
1 cup diced onion
1 cup diced celery
2 jalapeño peppers, seeded
   and finely diced
1 clove garlic, minced
1 teaspoon salt
1 teaspoon white pepper
1 teaspoon ground black pepper
1 teaspoon basil
1 teaspoon dried thyme
2 teaspoons fresh thyme
½ teaspoon garlic powder

½ cup veal stock (see index)
3 cups fish or chicken stock
   (see index)
1-2 tablespoons roux (see index)
½ teaspoon pepper sauce
   (Pickapeppa recommended)
2 teaspoons Worcestershire
   sauce
Cayenne pepper to taste
Tabasco sauce to taste
24 crawfish
1 teaspoon coriander
1 pound veal loin
Flour
2-3 tablespoons butter

1. Melt the margarine in a medium pot. Sauté the bell pepper, onion, and celery over medium high heat for 5 minutes. Reduce heat to medium and add the jalapeño, garlic, seasonings, and herbs. Cook another 5 minutes. Add the veal and fish or chicken stock. Bring to a boil over high heat. Reduce the heat and simmer. Stir in the roux. Add the pepper sauce and Worcestershire sauce. Add the cayenne and Tabasco to taste, about ¼ teaspoon cayenne and 2 to 3 dashes Tabasco. Simmer etouffée sauce for 30 minutes.

2. Remove the tails from 20 of the crawfish. Add the heads and claws to the simmering etouffée sauce. Cook the crawfish tails in boiling water seasoned with 1 teaspoon salt and the coriander for 4 to 5 minutes. Drain and reserve the tails.

3. Slice the veal in 8 pieces, about 2 ounces each. Place the veal between pieces of plastic wrap and pound into ⅛-inch thick medallions.

4. Lightly flour the veal. Sauté in melted butter over medium high heat, 30 seconds on each side. Reduce the heat to medium. Add the crawfish tails and sauté for another 20 seconds.

5. Arrange 2 veal medallions and 4 crawfish tails on each plate. Remove the crawfish heads and claws from the etouffée sauce and spoon over the meat. Garnish with a whole crawfish.

Eating crawfish tails can be tricky business. To facilitate removing the meat with a fork, before serving slice the tails lengthwise with a sharp knife, cracking but not severing the shell. To be authentic, eat the tail meat with fingers Bayou-style: grasp the tail end firmly and gently pull out the meat with your teeth.

JAMBALAYA RICE

4 tablespoons margarine	½ teaspoon basil
8 ounces smoked ham, diced	4 small bay leaves
8 ounces smoked sausage, diced	1 teaspoon salt
1 cup diced green bell pepper	¼ teaspoon cayenne
1 cup diced celery	2-3 dashes Tabasco sauce
1 cup chopped onion	8 ounces tomato sauce
1 teaspoon thyme	1½ cups rice
½ teaspoon oregano	1½ cups chicken stock (see index)

Melt the margarine in a large skillet over medium high heat. Add the ham and sausage; sauté for 5 minutes. Add the bell pepper, celery, onion, herbs, and seasonings. Cook, stirring occasionally, 8 to 10 minutes. Stir in the tomato sauce. Add the rice and cook 5 to 6 minutes. Add the stock and bring to a boil. Reduce the heat and simmer until the rice is tender, about 20 minutes. Remove bay leaves before serving.

HUSH PUPPIES

1 cup cornmeal
1 cup flour
1 egg
1 cup buttermilk
1 teaspoon fresh ground
  black pepper
½ teaspoon salt
⅛ teaspoon cayenne pepper

Pinch of garlic powder
½ teaspoon baking powder
4 scallions, green tops only,
  very finely chopped
1 tomato, peeled, seeded,
  and finely diced
Oil for deep frying

1. In a mixing bowl, thoroughly blend the cornmeal, flour, egg, and buttermilk. Add the black pepper, salt, cayenne, garlic powder, and baking powder. Blend well. Stir in the scallions and tomato.

2. Heat the oil to deep frying temperature. Drop the batter by teaspoonfuls into the hot oil. Fry until golden brown, about 1 minute on each side. Drain on paper towels. Fry the remaining batter. Serve warm.

CREOLE BREAD PUDDING with WHISKEY SAUCE

3 *large eggs*
1 *cup granulated sugar*
½ *cup brown sugar*
1½ *teaspoons vanilla extract*
1½ *teaspoons ground cinnamon*
1 *teaspoon ground nutmeg*
¼ *cup melted butter*

2 *cups light cream (half and half)*
½ *cup raisins*
½ *cup diced peaches*
5 *cups stale French or Italian bread, crusts on, in ¾-inch cubes*
WHISKEY SAUCE

1. In an electric mixer, beat the eggs on high speed until very frothy, about 3 minutes. Add the sugars, vanilla, cinnamon, nutmeg, and butter. Beat on high speed until well blended. Beat in the light cream. Stir in the raisins and peaches.

2. Place the bread cubes in a greased loaf pan. Pour the egg-cream mixture over the bread and stir well. Let the bread absorb the liquid, patting the bread down occasionally, for 45 minutes.

3. Bake in a 325° oven for 1 hour. Increase the temperature to 375° and bake for another 15 minutes until well browned.

4. To serve, spoon into dessert dishes and top with WHISKEY SAUCE.

WHISKEY SAUCE

2 *cups light cream (half and half)*
2 *teaspoons vanilla extract*

5 *egg yolks*
1 *cup sugar*
1-2 *ounces whiskey or to taste*

1. Over medium heat, slowly bring the light cream and vanilla to a boil, stirring frequently to prevent scorching.

2. Meanwhile, thoroughly blend the egg yolks and sugar.

3. As soon as the cream reaches a boil, remove from the heat. Slowly add the egg mixture, stirring constantly to prevent the eggs from cooking and becoming lumpy. Blend in the whiskey.

Bread Pudding with Whiskey Sauce is traditionally served warm. But it is also delicious served cold.

THE NEW YORKER

Dinner for Four

Lamb Sausage with Polenta and Tomato Sauce

Wild Mushroom Soup with Puff Pastry

Pike with Chive Sauce

Pear Tart with Honey Sauce

Wines:

With the Lamb Sausage and Polenta—Saintsbury Pinot Noir, Sonoma, 1982

With the Mushroom Soup—Eyrie Pinot Gris, 1982

With the Pike—Rodet Puligny Montrachet "Folatietres," 1981

With the Pear Tart—Chateau D'Yquem, Sauternes, 1976

Thomas Sieg and John Williams, Owners
Marco Schlenz, Chef-Proprietor
Will Pliler, Chef of the Kitchen

A pacesetter in area cuisine since its opening in 1978, the New Yorker offers patrons two distinctive dining experiences. Chef Marco Schlenz describes the cuisine of the main dining room, which features a sophisticated glass-and-brass decor and impeccable service, as "California-French, meaning that we use the freshest available ingredients and treat them with the most appropriate French and American techniques." In contrast with the formal dining room (whence comes the accompanying menu) is the section of the restaurant designated "an American cafe" where a separate menu offers modestly priced food in a strictly American vein—ranging from smoked pork chops, Maryland crab cakes, and maple syrup mousse to "all-American" salads, sandwiches, and French fries.

Whether the dining room or the cafe, the New Yorker cuisine bears the unmistakable imprint of its young chef. "My goal is to be an individualist, to stand out in the crowd, to be a leader from whom others borrow ideas. But I never seek strange or wierd food combinations just for the sake of doing it. I maintain a classical orientation with food and try to base everything on solid principles of cooking. My style is 'refined basic' in that we try to refine the simplest ingredients to the highest level." A native of Atlanta, Schlenz began his culinary career as a dishwasher at age 12 and quickly mastered all facets of kitchen service in restaurants across the country and at the Culinary Institute of America. "I have never deviated from the restaurant business because I love it. I enjoy the challenge of the kitchen. Out front you can offer the finest furnishings, service, wine, whatever, but it's all immaterial if what goes on the plate doesn't bring people back." Recently identified by *Food & Wine* magazine as one of the most "talented young chefs" in America, Schlenz is more than equal to the challenge.

The New Yorker is a private club offering annual as well as short-term memberships. Two seafood restaurants, The Oyster Bar (private) and the Market Street Grill (public), also housed in the old New Yorker hotel builing, are affiliates of the New Yorker Club.

60 Post Office Place   363-0166
Salt Lake City

LAMB SAUSAGE WITH POLENTA AND TOMATO SAUCE

LAMB SAUSAGE *Butter, about 2 tablespoons*
POLENTA *TOMATO SAUCE*

1. Place the LAMB SAUSAGES on a preheated grill or under a preheated broiler and cook to desired doneness, about 4 minutes for medium rare. Remove to a heated platter and keep warm.

2. Cut 4 slices of the POLENTA, about ½-inch thick. Melt 2 tablespoons of butter in a skillet over medium high heat. Sauté the POLENTA slices until hot and slightly browned.

3. While the POLENTA is sautéing, heat the TOMATO SAUCE but do not let it boil.

4. To serve, slice each LAMB SAUSAGE on the bias and arrange with slices overlapping in a semicircle on warmed plates. Place 1 square of fried POLENTA in front of each sausage. Nap with TOMATO SAUCE. Serve hot.

LAMB SAUSAGE

1 *pound lamb shoulder or leg,*   ½ *tablespoon finely minced*
  with fat cover intact   *garlic, or garlic purée*
1 *jalapeño pepper,*   *Salt*
  coarsely chopped   *Fresh ground black pepper*

1. Dice the lamb meat and fat into small cubes. Pass through a meat grinder using a medium die. Mix the jalapeño, garlic, and a sprinkling of salt and pepper with the ground lamb. Run the meat through the grinder a second time.

2. Cook a small portion of the lamb mixture, taste, and adjust seasonings if necessary.

3. Divide the lamb mixture into 4 equal parts. Shape each portion into a cylindrical sausage about 1-inch high, 1½-inches wide, and 4-inches long.

POLENTA

6 ounces unsalted butter
1 cup cornmeal, preferably Italian

3-4 cups rich chicken stock
(see index)
Salt to taste

1. Melt the butter over medium heat in a medium pot or large saucepan. Add the cornmeal and stir constantly until the butter is absorbed.

2. Meanwhile, bring the chicken stock to a boil. Add the boiling chicken stock, about 1 cup at at time, stirring constantly until the cornmeal has fully absorbed the stock and is smooth in consistency. Taste and season with salt if necessary.

3. Pour the hot polenta into a buttered terrine at least 3 inches deep (3x3x12 recommended). Cool, then refrigerate until serving time.

Sautéing the cornmeal in butter gives the polenta a special, nutty flavor. The same technique should be used with rice—always sauté rice in butter before adding hot water or stock for a much improved flavor.

TOMATO SAUCE

½ pound fresh plum tomatoes
1 tablespoon virgin olive oil

Salt
Fresh ground black pepper

Peel and seed the tomatoes. Purée the tomatoes in a food processor, slowly adding the olive oil while processing. Season with salt and pepper. Cook briefly over medium heat to evaporate excess liquid.

If fresh plum tomatoes are unavailable, use an equivalent amount of canned plum tomatoes or an 8-ounce can of good quality tomato sauce.

WILD MUSHROOM SOUP WITH PUFF PASTRY

½ pound each of 3 types of
   domestic wild mushrooms
   (chanterelles, oysters, porcini)
8 cups rich chicken or veal stock
   (see index)
4 cups heavy (whipping) cream
1 teaspoon finely minced shallots

¼ pound plus 2 tablespoons
   unsalted butter
½ cup dry vermouth
   Salt and white pepper
1 sheet commercial puff pastry
1 egg
2 tablespoons water

1. Wash and slice the mushrooms. Set aside.

2. Boil the chicken or veal stock until reduced by one-half. Add the cream and reduce by one-half.

3. While the stock and cream mixture is reducing, in a separate pan sauté the shallots in ¼ pound butter until translucent. Add the mushrooms and vermouth and cook until the mushrooms are soft. Add the shallots and mushrooms to the stock and cream mixture and simmer until the mushroom essence is extracted, 15 to 35 minutes. Season with salt and pepper to taste. While still warm, swirl in the remaining 2 tablespoons unsalted butter. Cool.

4. Fill oven-proof soup cups no more than ¾ full with the cooled soup. Cut 4 circles ½-inch larger in diameter than the soup cups from the puff pastry sheet. Place a circle of puff pastry atop each soup bowl and press edges of the circle to the sides of the cup to adhere securely. Combine the egg and water and brush over the surface of the puff pastry. Bake in a preheated 400° oven until the crust is golden and doubled in height, 10 to 15 minutes. Serve immediately.

It is essential that the soup is cooled before covering with puff pastry and that the soup cups are no more than ¾ full. If the soup is too warm, the pastry will sag; if the cup is too full, the bubbling soup will soak the crust while baking.

PIKE WITH CHIVE SAUCE

Salt and pepper
4 (8-ounce) boned filets pike
   (or sea bass or other firm-
   fleshed white fish)
   Flour for dusting
3 tablespoons oil
¼ cup vermouth
1½ cups fish stock (see index)

1 tablespoon minced shallots
1 cup heavy (whipping) cream
   Juice of 1 lemon
3 tablespoons chopped fresh
   chives
4 tablespoons unsalted butter
   Chopped parsley for garnish

1. Salt, pepper, and dust the filets in flour. Heat the oil in a skillet over high heat. Sear the filets until golden brown on each side, no more than 3 to 4 minutes total. Transfer the skillet to a preheated 400° or 425° oven until the flesh is just opaque, no more than 4 to 5 minutes. Remove the filets to a heated platter and keep warm while making the sauce.

2. Pour off the excess oil from the skillet and return to high heat. Deglaze the skillet with the vermouth. Add the fish stock, shallots, and cream. Reduce by half. Add salt and pepper to taste. Add the lemon juice and chives. Adjust seasonings. Remove the skillet from the heat and slowly incorporate the butter, blending with a whisk. Adjust seasonings.

3. To serve, spoon a layer of chive sauce on serving plates. Place the filets on top of the sauce. Garnish with chopped parsley.

At the New Yorker this entrée would be accompanied by a medley of baby vegetables, steamed or sautéed whole. The treatment is simple because baby vegetables have a unique, sweet flavor and need only to be cooked until tender.

A recipe is only a guideline. The cardinal rule to cooking is taste, taste, and taste again.

PEAR TART with HONEY SAUCE

Flaky pie dough
(your favorite recipe)
4 *ripe pears*
Sugar
Cinnamon

4 *tablespoons unsalted butter,*
cut into small dice
1 *cup honey*
4 *tablespoons unsalted butter*
Mint leaves for garnish

1. Roll out the pie dough to a thickness of ⅛-inch. Cut into 4 circles, each about 4-inches in diameter. Place the circles of dough on an ungreased cookie or baking sheet.

2. Peel, stem, and core the pears. Cut into ¼-inch thick slices. Fan out the slices of 1 pear to cover 1 circle of dough. Sprinkle the pears with sugar and cinnamon to taste. Distribute diced butter over the pears.

3. Bake the tarts in a preheated 350° oven until the crust is golden brown, 5 to 7 minutes.

4. While the tarts are baking, heat the honey and butter in a small saucepan. Blend well.

5. To serve, cover the bottom of a heated plate with a thin layer of the warm honey sauce. Place a pear tart on the sauce. Garnish with mint leaves. Serve hot.

RESTAURANT

Dinner for Four

Cozze Ripieni

Guanciali

Scallopini di Vitello alla Marsala

Zabaglione Freddo con Frutta

Cenci alla Maurizio

Wines:

With the First Courses—Santa Margherita Pinot Grigio

With the Entrée—Corvo Duca di Salaparuta

Antonino and Jouvina Carilli, Owners

Maurice Sainte-Yves, Chef

Located high above the city on the twenty-fourth floor of the University Club Building, Nino's is an extraordinary dining spot. The view is magnificent, a commanding panorama of the city and mountains. The decor is tastefully elegant—wood paneling, upholstered chairs, pastel linens, tiered seating. Most important, the featured Northern Italian cuisine is a delight to the eye as well as the palate.

Chef Maurice resides over a kitchen with a view as expansive as his cuisine. A proponent of nuova cucina in preparation and presentation of foods, the personal signature of this culinary artist is visible in every dish. His credo is freshness—fresh ingredients, fresh tastes, fresh textures. He cooks with a light hand, favoring delicate sauces and seasonings. And he has a strong bias against the excessive use of salt, sugar, and flour. His style is to treat natural foods in a simple manner. A pioneer in introducing Northern Italian cuisine to the city, Maurice has worked hard to counter the public's tendency to equate the cooking of Southern Italy with "Italian food." He is a effecting a revolution in dining habits with such specialities as Gamberi Marinate, Pansoti alla Panna, Calamari Ripieni con Funghi, and Pollo alla Griglia al Rosmarino.

Nino's is owned and managed by the Carilli family, restaurateurs in the San Francisco Bay area since the early 1950s. In addition to Nino's, the Carillis currently own Antonino's Restaurant in Hayward, California. They were drawn to Utah by the area's growth potential. "Salt Lake City is a rapidly growing community with increased emphasis on fine dining. We are pleased to be part of it."

University Club Building   355-3456
136 East South Temple
Salt Lake City

COZZE RIPIENI

12 fresh mussels	½ teaspoon minced garlic
6 tablespoons bread crumbs	2 tablespoons olive oil
3 tablespoons finely chopped red onion	3-4 tablespoons chicken stock
	Red radicchio
	Seaweed for garnish

1. Scrub and debeard the mussels. Without breaking the hinge, open the mussel shells over the bread crumbs so that the crumbs absorb the juices. Set aside.

2. Sauté the onion and garlic in the olive oil until soft and translucent, 3 to 4 minutes. Add the bread crumbs, stirring to combine well. Slowly add the chicken stock until the bread crumb mixture adheres but is not too wet. Let cool to lukewarm.

3. When the stuffing has cooled, place about 1 teaspoon inside each mussel. Close the shells and secure tightly with kitchen twine or heavy string by wrapping the string around the mussel 3 or 4 times. Steam the mussels for 4 minutes.

4. To serve, remove the string and open the shells slightly to resemble a butterfly. Arrange 3 mussels per person on a bed of red radicchio. Garnish with seaweed if available.

There are two simple, but critical, steps in the preparation of this dish. First, you must not add too much chicken stock to the stuffing mixture or it will not absorb the mussel juices while steaming. It is better that the stuffing be a little dry than too moist. Second, the mussels must be tied tightly or the steam will saturate the stuffing while cooking.

Red onions are preferred because of their mild, sweet taste, but white or yellow onions may be substituted.

GUANCIALI

PASTA DOUGH
1 egg beaten with
 1 teaspoon water
CHEESE FILLING
Salt

TOMATO AND MUSHROOM
 SAUCE
Grated Parmesan cheese,
 as needed
Fresh ground black pepper
 (optional)

1. Roll out the PASTA DOUGH to a thickness of ¹⁄₁₆-inch. Trim the rough edges to form a square. Cut the square in half. Brush the entire surface of one sheet of the dough with the egg wash. Place ½ teaspoon of the CHEESE FILLING in rows at regular intervals, about 2 inches apart, across the sheet. Cover with the second sheet of dough, pressing firmly around the edges of the sheet and around each portion of the CHEESE FILLING to seal. With a knife or ravioli cutter, separate into individual pillows. Trim rough edges if any. If using a knife, press edges of the pillows with the tines of a fork to seal. Let rest 30 minutes before cooking.

2. Drop the ravioli into boiling, salted water. Reduce the heat and cook at a moderate boil for 5 to 7 minutes. Drain.

3. Divide the ravioli among 4 plates. Serve with TOMATO AND MUSHROOM SAUCE topped with grated Parmesan cheese and fresh ground black pepper.

There is only one sure way to tell if pasta is cooked properly—"al dente," tender yet a little firm to the bite. Taste it!

PASTA DOUGH

¾ cup all-purpose flour
¼ cup semolina flour
1 teaspoon olive oil

1 extra large egg,
   room temperature
½ teaspoon salt

Combine the flour and semolina on a pastry board or other smooth work surface. Make a well in the center. Add the olive oil, egg, and salt. With a fork, lightly beat the egg while slowly incorporating the flour. Knead 3 to 4 minutes until the dough is smooth and soft, but not sticky. Cover with plastic wrap and let rest at room temperature for 1 hour.

There can be no precise recipe for pasta dough or bread because the amount of liquid and flour needed varies with the temperature, humidity, and the milling of the flour. The size and temperature of the egg will also influence the amount of flour that can be absorbed. You simply must go by feel. If the pasta dough seems too sticky, add additional flour. If it seems too dry, add water, 1 tablespoon at a time.

CHEESE FILLING

½ cup ricotta cheese
1 teaspoon finely chopped
   parsley or spinach

1 egg yolk
¼ teaspoon freshly grated nutmeg
1 tablespoon grated Parmesan
   or Asiago cheese

Combine the ricotta and parsley or spinach. Add the egg yolk and nutmeg. Blend well. Stir in the Parmesan or Asiago cheese. Set aside.

I try to avoid the use of salt whenever possible. For almost every dish there is an ingredient that can serve as a salt substitute. In this case, the saltiness of the Parmesan or Asiago cheese serves as the seasoning.

TOMATO AND MUSHROOM SAUCE

1 cup sliced mushrooms
½ teaspoon minced garlic
2 tablespoons olive oil
½ cup diced tomato,
    skinned but not seeded

½ cup chicken stock
4 ounces unsalted butter,
    room temperature
1 teaspoon chopped parsley

Sauté the mushrooms and garlic in the olive oil for 2 minutes over medium heat. Add the tomatoes and cook another 2 minutes. Add the chicken stock and cook 3 minutes. Off the heat, stir in the butter 2 tablespoons at a time. Stir in the parsley just before serving.

In keeping with the spirit of fresh taste and texture, do not remove the seeds from the tomato. Only the French remove tomato seeds from everything.

SCALLOPINI DI VITELLO ALLA MARSALA

1¼ pounds veal tenderloin
   Flour
4 tablespoons clarified butter
⅓ cup dry Marsala

1 cup sliced mushrooms
½ cup brown veal stock
   (see index)
6 tablespoons unsalted butter

1. Slice the veal tenderloin into 8 pieces, 2½ ounces each. Pound each piece between plastic wrap into ⅛-inch thick scallopini. Lightly flour scallopini on one side only. Sauté, flour side down, in the clarified butter for no more than 30 seconds on each side. Remove the scallopini to a heated platter and keep warm.

2. Add the Marsala to the skillet to deglaze. Add the mushrooms and veal stock. Simmer until the liquid is reduced by about one-third. Off the heat, stir in the butter, 2 tablespoons at a time. Return the veal to the skillet and reheat slightly in the sauce.

3. Serve 2 scallopini per person well covered with mushroom sauce.

Technically, picatta come from the tenderloin, scallopini from the leg. The tenderloin is much more tender, so we use it for both.

If the butter does not incorporate well or begins to separate from the sauce, there is insufficient liquid to hold the heavy butter fat. Add more stock until the butter holds.

ZABAGLIONE FREDDO CON FRUTTA

3 large egg yolks	1 pint fresh raspberries
¼ cup sugar	1 pint fresh blackberries
¼ cup dry Marsala	

1. Whisk the egg yolks and sugar in a stainless steel bowl until the sugar is well incorporated. Stir in the Marsala.

2. Fill a pot slightly larger than the steel bowl with enough water to reach the bottom of the steel bowl. Bring the water to a steady simmer, but not a boil. Place the steel bowl over the pot with the bottom just touching the water. Whisk the egg mixture constantly until it becomes light and creamy and retains soft peaks, 2 to 3 minutes.

3. Serve immediately or chilled over berries divided among dessert goblets.

Zabaglione can be cooked over direct heat, but it is tricky to avoid solidifying the eggs. A regular double boiler does not give enough surface area for the vigorous whisking necessary for a light and creamy Zabaglione. A makeshift double boiler, bowl or pan over a pot, works best.

A dessert need not be elaborate to be effective, but it must be appropriate. That is, the dessert should be on a plateau above the entrée to be a fitting climax to the meal. The more elaborate the entrée, the more elaborate the dessert. Each dish in the meal should reach a higher plateau.

CENCI ALLA MAURIZIO

PASTA DOUGH as for Guanciali
1 large or 2 medium straw-
    berries, 5 raspberries, or
    ½ banana per person

Toothpicks
Oil for deep frying
Confectioners sugar
Cinnamon

Roll out the pasta dough as thinly as possible. Cut into 4 rectangles, 4 x 6 inches. Place the fruit in the middle of the dough. Lift the top and bottom (short sides) and then the sides over the fruit filling. Press the dough together to seal and then secure with a toothpick. Deep fry until golden brown. Dust with the confectioners sugar and sprinkle with cinnamon.

It is important that the pasta dough be rolled as thin as possible: the thinner the dough, the more delicate the cenci. When sealing the fruit in the dough, it may be helpful to pretend the rectangle is a round Chinese dumpling wrapper. The shape of the dough to be filled is optional. The dough can be cut into circles, rectangles, or ravioli-like squares. The concept, not the shape, is important.

philippe's
at the Copperbottom Inn
Park City, Utah

Dinner for Six

Foie de Canard Chaud Vinaigrette

Escalope de Saumon au Citron Vert

Filet de Porc au Calvados

Tomate aux Herbes

Courgette à l'Aneth

Pommes Gratinée Forêzienne

Tourte au Chocolat et Cerises Noires

Wine:

Fendant, Grand Vin du Valais, Caves Mövenpick, 1982
(a Swiss white wine)

Philippe Held, Owner-Chef

"Philippe's is my personal fulfillment," says Philippe Held of his Park City restaurant. The Swiss-born chef, who has cooked in famous kitchens in Europe and has operated restaurants in Sun Valley and Aspen, came to Utah determined "to stay out of kitchen." But the "creativity of food preparation and the challenge of trying to please people" led him to take over the vacant coffee shop in the Copperbottom Inn in December, 1981. The talented chef has successfully combated the boredom of routine by completely changing his diverse menu each week despite the considerable effort required to coordinate new ideas with product availability.

Philippe describes his cuisine as classical and innovative but oriented toward the provincial side of French cooking. He is emphatic about the use of fresh herbs and local products whenever possible. Although he shuns starches and favors light sauces, Philippe does not follow la nouvelle cuisine in preparation or presentation. The reason is pragmatic rather than culinary. "People who ski all day need calories, so we serve hearty portions at very reasonable prices. I want people to leave satisfied with the quality and sufficiency of their meal." The sensitivity to the great out-of-doors environment carries over into the restaurant's decor as the warm tones of burnt orange and natural wood along with an open hearth fireplace create an atmosphere of conviviality and relaxed formality.

"My goal," confides Philippe as he contemplates expansion of the facility, "is for people from all over the country to talk about a great restaurant in Park City. We are getting better and better and keep moving toward perfection." Utahns would say that he has already reached that goal. So, too, would the Gourmet Diner's Club of America, which honored Philippe's with the Silver Spoon Award in 1983 and 1984.

Copperbottom Inn   649-2421
1637 Shortline Road
Park City

FOIE DE CANARD CHAUD VINAIGRETTE

½ pound fresh foie gras
Salt
Fresh ground black pepper

Flour
BALSAMIC VINAIGRETTE

1. Slice the foie gras into 6 pieces, ½-inch thick. Sprinkle both sides with salt and pepper. Lightly flour each piece, shaking off any excess.
2. Over medium heat, sauté the foie gras in a dry, non-stick pan for 25 to 30 seconds on each side.
3. Serve 1 slice per person topped with warm BALSAMIC VINAIGRETTE.

BALSAMIC VINAIGRETTE

2 tablespoons minced shallots
½ cup Balsamic vinegar
2 tablespoons chopped chives
2 tablespoons minced chervil
    (1½ tablespoons dried)

2 tablespoons minced parsley
⅓ cup walnut oil
Salt
Fresh ground pepper

In a skillet over medium heat, warm the shallots in the vinegar for 1 minute. Add the fresh herbs and cook for 30 seconds. Add the walnut oil and cook for another 30 seconds. Add salt and pepper to taste. Add more walnut oil if too tart. Keep warm while preparing the foie gras.

ESCALOPE DE SAUMON AU CITRON VERT

1 *cup white wine*
½ *cup vermouth*
2 *cups heavy (whipping) cream*
  Juice of ½ lime
  Salt and white pepper

3 *tablespoons clarified butter*
6 *(4-ounce) salmon filets,*
  about ½-inch thick
6 *slices kiwi, ⅛-inch thick*
3 *thin lime slices, halved*

1. Bring the wine and vermouth to a boil in a non-aluminum pan and let reduce over medium heat to a thin syrup, about ⅓ to ½ cup. Add the cream and let reduce until the wine-cream sauce is thick and has a bright sheen, about 1 ample cup. Add the lime juice. Add a pinch of salt and white pepper if needed.

2. Meanwhile, heat the clarified butter in a large, heavy skillet with a heat-proof handle over medium heat. Lightly salt and pepper the salmon filets and sauté briefly, 15 to 20 seconds each side. Place them under the broiler to finish cooking, 5 to 6 minutes. The exterior flesh of the salmon should be translucent and beginning to flake while the center is still slightly pink.

3. Serve 1 salmon filet per person topped with cream sauce. Garnish with 1 kiwi slice and ½ lime slice.

FILET DE PORC AU CALVADOS

3 *whole pork tenderloins*
  Salt
  Oil for cooking
2 *large apples (Golden Delicious*
  or Granny Smith), peeled
  and cored

2 *tablespoons butter*
2 *tablespoons fresh tarragon*
  leaves, in 1-inch pieces
¼ *cup Calvados*
¾ *cup veal stock (see index)*

1. Trim the tenderloins of excess fat. Lightly salt.

2. In a heavy skillet, warm a thin film of oil over high heat. Brown the tenderloins, separately if necessary, on all sides until lightly browned, about 5 minutes. Finish cooking in a hot (425°) oven, turning once, until nicely browned, 15 to 20 minutes. Set aside while cooking the apples.

3. Cut the apples into ¼-inch slices. Sauté in butter over medium heat until just tender, about 5 minutes. Add the tarragon and Calvados. Ignite. When the flame is extinguished, add the veal stock. Cook about 1 minute until warmed through.

4. Cut the tenderloins into ¼-inch slices on the bias. Served topped with apples.

TOMATE AUX HERBES

3 *medium tomatoes*	2 *teaspoons minced fresh thyme*
Salt and fresh ground pepper	2 *teaspoons minced fresh basil*
2 *teaspoons minced fresh*	2 *tablespoons melted butter*
rosemary	2 *tablespoons butter*

1. Slice the tomatoes in half horizontally and cut out the stem core. Sprinkle each tomato half with salt, pepper, and herbs. Drizzle with melted butter.

2. Melt the remaining 2 tablespoons butter in a medium skillet with a heat-poof handle. Place the seasoned tomato halves in the skillet and bake in a hot (400°) oven for 6 to 7 minutes.

COURGETTE À L'ANETH

2 *medium zucchini*	1 *tablespoon chopped fresh dill*
2-3 *tablespoons butter*	*Salt and white pepper*

Trim the ends of the zucchini and slice into ⅛-inch thick pieces. Sauté in butter over medium heat until crisp-tender, 4 to 5 minutes. Sprinkle with dill and salt and white pepper to taste.

POMMES GRATINÉE FORÊZIENNE

3 medium baking potatoes	1 clove garlic, finely minced
2 tablespoons melted butter	1 pint heavy (whipping) cream
Salt and white pepper	

1. Peel the potatoes and cut into ⅛-inch thick slices. Coat the bottom and sides of a shallow oven-proof serving dish with the melted butter.

2. Layer the potatoes in the baking dish. Sprinkle the potatoes with the salt, pepper, and garlic. Pour the cream over the potatoes.

3. Cover the baking dish with aluminum foil pierced with 2 or 3 small holes to release steam. Bake in a 400° oven until the potatoes are tender, about 60 minutes.

The success of this simple but delicious dish depends on layering the potatoes and then topping with the other ingredients. If the dish is stirred after the cream is added, the potato starch will not be able to bind the slices together. The idea is to allow the potatoes to absorb the cream while baking so as to produce a smooth, creamy texture.

TOURTE AU CHOCOLAT ET CERISES NOIRES

MARINATED CHERRIES:

2 pounds fresh or 30 ounces canned dark sweet cherries, pitted

½ cup sugar
1 cup water
¼ cup Kirsch

1. If using canned cherries, drain. Save the liquid for another use.

2. Bring the sugar and water to a boil over medium heat, stirring until the sugar is dissolved. Let cook for 3 minutes. Stir in the Kirsch. Add the cherries and marinate overnight.

CAKE:

6 ounces hazelnuts (filberts), finely chopped
6 ounces blanched almonds, finely chopped

2 tablespoons cocoa powder
2 ounces unsweetened chocolate, grated
10 eggs, separated
1 cup sugar

1. Mix together the nuts, cocoa powder, and grated chocolate. Set aside.

2. With an electric mixer or wire whisk, beat the 10 egg whites with ½ cup sugar to the stiff peak stage. Set aside.

3. In a large mixing bowl, beat the 10 egg yolks and the remaining ½ cup sugar until the mixture forms ribbons when the beaters or whisk is raised.

4. Gently fold the egg whites and nuts, ⅓ at a time, into the egg yolk mixture. Do not over mix.

5. Divide the batter between two 9-inch cake pans (springform recommended) that have been greased and floured or lined with parchment paper. Bake in a preheated 350° oven for 35 minutes. Remove the cakes from the pans and cool on a wire rack.

FILLING:
    MARINATED CHERRIES
    4 ounces semisweet chocolate

4 cups heavy (whipping) cream
3 tablespoons Kirsch
¼ cup confectioners sugar

1. Drain the cherries and set aside. Reserve the Kirsch syrup.
2. Melt the chocolate in the top of a double boiler. Reserve.
3. With an electric mixer or wire whisk, whip the cream with the Kirsch and powdered sugar until firm. Remove 1½ cups of the cream to another bowl. Reserve the remainder.
4. Gently fold the melted chocolate into 1½ cups of the whipped cream. Spoon chocolate cream into a pastry bag with a round tip.

To Assemble the Torte:

1. Slice one of the cake rounds in half horizontally.
2. Brush the whole cake round with the Kirsch syrup. Pipe on a layer of chocolate cream. Arrange about half of the cherries at regular intervals in concentric circles from the perimeter to the center of the cake.
3. Brush one of the half-layers of cake with the Kirsch syrup. Place on the layer of filling. Repeat the piping of chocolate cream and distribution of cherries as in Step 2.
4. Place the remaining half-layer of cake on the second layer of filling. Frost the entire torte with the remaining whipped cream. Garnish with additional cherries and chocolate shavings.

This light, delicious version of the famous Black Forest Cake is the creation of my talented pastry chef, Roxanne Greene.

Dinner for Four

Crêpe aux Escargots et aux Petits Légumes

Soupe Glacée aux Concombres

Filet Mignon Madagascar

Purée de Courge

Sorbet aux Framboises

Wines:

With the Crêpes—Laboure-Roi Pouilly-Fuisse, 1980

With the Filets—Corton Clos du Roi, 1978

Lottie Ann Van Dongen, Owner-Manager

Drew Ellsworth, Owner-Chef

Restaurant Dijon

T he exposed adobe bricks and pioneer architecture of a century-old country mansion combine with elegantly framed tableaux to create a unique French gallery ambiance for patrons of Restaurant Dijon. Chef Drew Ellsworth, who studied with André Doré at Le Vinarium in Dijon and with Paul Bocuse at his famous restaurant near Lyon, specializes in the classic cuisine of Burgundy. The menu also includes well known dishes from other famous gastronomic regions of France. "In preparing French regional food, we have meticulously sought authenticity. At the same time, we fully realize the limitations in serving a foreign cuisine in America. We do not serve exotic or bizarre dishes or add American touches to traditional French recipes. Our goal is to carefully select a cuisine which in its natural, authentic state is easily enjoyed by American palates."

Although Jambon Persillé, Soupe à l'oignon gratinée, and Truite Bocuse remain the most popular specialties of the house, Chef Ellsworth leans heavily in presentation toward the principles of la nouvelle cuisine, especially in fish dishes.

Established in 1979, Restaurant Dijon, in the great European tradition, is a "restaurant de famille" owned and operated by Chef Ellsworth and his sister, Lottie Ann Van Dongen. They also operate the Ecole Dijon school of French cookery.

4678 Highland Drive   272-5412
Salt Lake City

CRÊPE AUX ESCARGOTS ET AUX PETIT LÉGUMES

4 tablespoons butter	2 teaspoons capers
2-3 teaspoons finely chopped garlic	⅛ teaspoon sweet basil
2-3 teaspoons finely chopped shallots	⅛ teaspoon thyme
24 large escargots	⅛ teaspoon ground bay leaf
1 medium carrot, cut into 1½-inch thin julienne strips	Scant pinch cayenne pepper
	½ teaspoon lemon juice
1 large leek, white part only, cut into 1½-inch thin julienne strips	½ cup white wine
	Salt and white pepper to taste
½ medium green pepper, cut into 1½-inch thin julienne strips	4 (8- or 9-inch) dinner CRÊPES, warmed
	Parsley or dill for garnish

1. In a large sauté pan, melt the butter over high heat until it begins to turn blond. Add garlic and shallots and sauté for 1 minute. Add all other ingredients except the wine and sauté for 1 more minute. Add the wine and cook 1 more minute. Adjust seasonings, adding salt and white pepper to taste.

2. Divide the escargots and vegetable mixture among the 4 CRÊPES on individual warm plates. Pour cooking liquid over and around the CRÊPES. Garnish with parsley.

CRÊPES

2 cups milk
2 eggs
1 teaspoon sugar
½ teaspoon salt

1 cup flour
4 tablespoons butter, melted
2 tablespoons oil

1. In an electric mixer, blender, or food processor or with a wire whisk, beat the milk, eggs, sugar, and salt until frothy. Gradually add the flour while continuing to beat. Add the butter and beat until well incorporated.

2. Heat the oil in a 8- or 9-inch diameter pan, preferably non-stick, until very hot. Pour off any excess oil and add ¼ cup of the batter. Immediately lift the pan off the flame and quickly swirl the batter to coat the bottom. Return to heat and cook for about 30 seconds or until the crêpe begins to pull away from the edges of the pan. Turn to cook the other side.

3. Repeat with remaining batter. Use immediately or stack crêpes and refrigerate or freeze until needed. Warm before using.

The first crêpe is almost always a disaster, so don't worry if it burns or tears. The frothier the batter is beaten, the lighter the crêpes. It is also very important to stir the batter each time before adding more to the pan in order to keep the butter well blended. Cooking crêpes goes a lot faster if you use a second pan, preferably an electric skillet, to cook the second side. This recipe makes 15 to 16 crêpes and can be halved or doubled. For dessert crêpes add more sugar. Crêpes freeze very well.

SOUPE GLACÉE AUX CONCOMBRES

1 medium cucumber, seeded,
  peeled, and coarsely chopped
1 medium cucumber, seeded
  and coarsely chopped
1 large bell pepper,
  coarsely chopped
1 shallot, chopped
¼ teaspoon dill weed or 1 fresh
  sprig of dill
2 (1-inch thick) slices dry
  French bread (baguette size)

1 cup half and half
1 cup milk
2 tablespoons olive oil
2 tablespoons red wine vinegar
  Dash of Tabasco sauce
  Splash of lemon juice
  Salt and white pepper to taste
  Diced cucumber for garnish
  Diced red bell pepper for garnish

Combine all ingredients in a blender or food processor. Blend until smooth and creamy. Chill for a least 3 to 4 hours before serving. Serve cold with diced cucumber or diced red bell pepper for garnish.

The bread is important for texture. If French bread is not available, substitute any other white bread. If soup thickens too much while chilling, thin with water (not milk) just before serving.

FILET MIGNON MADAGASCAR

4 *teaspoons green (Madagascar)*
   peppercorns
4 *(8-ounce) tenderloin steaks*
   Salt and white pepper to taste

¼ *cup brandy*
½ *cup sour cream*
½ *cup heavy (whipping) cream*
1 *tablespoon Dijon mustard*
   Chopped parsley for garnish

1. Several hours (3 to 4) before preparation, press peppercorns into both sides of steaks. Refrigerate until 30 minutes before cooking. Remove from refrigerator and bring to room temperature.

2. Sprinkle steaks with salt and cook to desired doneness in a heavy, lightly oiled skillet. Remove from the skillet and place in a warmed oven while making sauce.

3. Pour off any excess oil from the pan and pat dry with paper toweling. Over high heat add brandy to deglaze the pan, rapidly scraping up any browned bits of meat. Reduce heat to medium low. Add the sour cream, heavy cream, and mustard. Combine with a wire whisk. Let cream reduce to desired consistency. Add salt and pepper to taste.

4. Serve steaks topped with brandy/cream sauce. Garnish with chopped parsley.

French cream has a slightly sour taste similar to crème fraiche. An acceptable substitute is equal parts sour cream and heavy cream.

PURÉE DE COURGE

3½ cups hot steamed banana
    squash, cut in chunks
2 tablespoons butter
⅓ cup sour cream
½ teaspoon white pepper

Salt to taste
⅛ teaspoon freshly ground
    nutmeg
1 tablespoon finely chopped
    shallots

In a food processor or mixing bowl combine all ingredients. Blend until thoroughly combined. Adjust seasonings and serve hot.

SORBET AUX FRAMBOISES

4 cups whole frozen raspberries
¼ cup orange liqueur,
    preferably Grand Marnier

⅓ cup sugar
½ cup heavy (whipping) cream
1 tablespoon fresh lemon juice

Combine all ingredients in a food processor and blend until smooth but still in an iced state. Serve immediately or place in a freezer container and serve within the hour.

It is essential that whole, individually frozen berries be used in making the sorbet. Berries frozen into blocks with syrup simply will not work because they must be thawed before processing and will quickly turn to ice when refrozen. If fresh berries are used, they must be individually frozen.

the Roof

Dinner for Four

Mussels à la Poulette

Gazpacho

Belgian Endive Salad with Walnut Oil Dressing

*Noisettes of Lamb with Artichoke,
Tomato Concasser, Braised Leeks, and Basil Cream Sauce*

Profiteroles au Chocolat

Wines:

With the Mussels—Chalone Pinot Blanc, 1980

With the Lamb—Acacia Pinot Noir, St. Clair, 1980

Roger Cortello, Executive Chef

Charles Wiley, Chef de Cuisine

THE ROOF

When the Hotel Utah opened in 1911, the national trade magazine *Hotel Monthly* remarked that the roof garden restaurant overlooking Temple Square "will doubtless prove a great attraction, for both guests of the hotel and residents of the city." The assessment was correct. For nearly three-quarters of a century, the tenth-floor restaurant of the Hotel Utah—whether called the Roof Garden, the Starlite Roof, the Sky Room, or simply the The Roof—has been a nationally acclaimed dining landmark in Salt Lake City.

The decor and cuisine have changed periodically to keep current with the culinary times, but the restaurant has consistently offered its patrons superb food along with a spectacular view of city, mountains, and the Great Salt Lake. Today, The Roof serves American and Continental cuisine in a setting of understated elegance. Woodpaneled walls, subdued pastel and earth-tone colors, tables dressed in white linen, and service personnel in black ties evoke an atmosphere of tradition and good taste at both luncheon and dinner. Tiered seating maximizes the panoramic view of the city's western skyline.

The Roof is the first restaurant in Utah to receive *Travel/Holiday* magazine's highest dining award, an honor bestowed annually since 1978. Responsible for the award-winning cuisine is Executive Chef Roger Cortello, a professional member of the Chaine des Rotisseurs and a founder of the Beehive Chefs Association. Chef Charles Wiley emphasizes presentation as well as preparation of fine food. Wiley has four cardinal points of reference when cooking for The Roof. "Using contemporary ideas while maintaining the roots of classic French cuisine is important. So is the regular featuring of new and varied items on the menu to create exciting dining. We are also committed to using the freshest ingredients available, especially herbs and seafood, and feel that attention to contrast in color, texture, and flavor is all-important in planning a menu."

Originally owned and operated by the Mormon Church, the Hotel Utah came under the management of the Westin Hotel corporation in 1984.

Westin Hotel Utah   531-1000
Main at South Temple
Salt Lake City

MUSSELS À LA POULETTE

48 *fresh mussels*
2 *shallots, finely diced*
2 *cloves garlic, minced*
2 *teaspoons butter*
  Pinch of thyme,
    fresh if available

Pinch of salt and white pepper
1 *teaspoon chopped parsley*
1 *bay leaf*
1 *cup dry white wine*
4 *tablespoons heavy (whipping)*
  cream

1. Debeard and clean the mussels.
2. In a saucepan large enough to hold the mussels, sauté the shallots and garlic in butter over medium heat until translucent. Be careful not to discolor or brown the garlic.
3. Add the remaining ingredients and cook, covered, over high heat until the mussels open (about 2 minutes).
4. Divide the mussels among individual serving bowls, discarding any mussels that did not open. Pour sauce over the mussels and serve immediately.

To clean mussels, scrub with a stiff brush and submerge in salted water for at least 6 hours to remove sand. It may be necessary to cook the mussels in two batches. If so, divide the recipe and cook two batches simultaneously.

GAZPACHO

2 cups canned stewed tomatoes,
   with juice
½ cup canned tomato juice
1 large green pepper,
   finely chopped
1 large cucumber, seeded
   and finely chopped
½ Bermuda (red) onion,
   finely chopped

2 cloves garlic,
   very finely chopped
1 cup beef broth
   (canned is acceptable)
¼ cup olive oil
3 tablespoons red wine vinegar
½ teaspoon Worcestershire sauce
   Dash of Tabasco
   Salt to taste
   Croutons as needed for garnish

1. Strain the stewed tomatoes; reserve the juice. Chop the pulp finely.
2. Combine remaining ingredients with the tomato pulp and reserved tomato juice. Adjust seasonings. Chill at least 2 hours before serving.
3. Top each serving with croutons if desired.

Fresh tomatoes in season may be substituted for canned tomatoes. If using fresh tomatoes, peel and seed before finely chopping the pulp. Add 1½ cups canned tomato juice.

Chef Wiley prefers the chunky and crisp texture of hand-chopped vegetables to the puréed effect produced by a food processor.

BELGIAN ENDIVE SALAD
WITH WALNUT OIL DRESSING

2 *large or 3 small Belgian endives*	¼ *cup chopped walnuts*
1 *bunch watercress*	*WALNUT OIL DRESSING*

1. Separate endive spears by cutting off the heel. Wash in cold water and pat dry.
2. Repeat this process for the watercress. Trim off stems.
3. Reserve 16 spears of endive and cut the rest into 1-inch squares.
4. Toss the endive and watercress separately with WALNUT OIL DRESSING until the leaves are barely coated with the dressing.
5. Arrange the endive spears and watercress in a symmetrical pattern around the edge of serving plate. Fill the center of the plate with the cut endive. Top with chopped walnuts.

WALNUT OIL DRESSSING

1 *teaspoon Dijon mustard*	*Salt and white pepper to taste*
½ *teaspoon extrafine sugar*	½ *cup tarragon vinegar*
	1½ *cups walnut oil*

1. Combine the mustard, sugar, a pinch of salt and pepper, and the vinegar in a mixing bowl. Beat briefly with a wire whisk.
2. Gradually add the oil in a thin stream, whisking constantly until well blended. Adjust seasonings.

Makes 2 cups.

NOISETTES OF LAMB WITH ARTICHOKE, TOMATO CONCASSER, BRAISED LEEKS, AND BASIL CREAM SAUCE

4   racks of lamb
4   leeks
1   quart plus 6 cups water
4   teaspoons salt
4   artichokes
1   lemon, quartered
¼   cup flour

¼   cup lemon juice
    TOMATO CONCASSER
2   cups BASIL CREAM SAUCE
1   cup chicken broth
    Salt and pepper to taste
    Olive oil as needed

1. Remove the eye from the rack of lamb, leaving the shank portion attached. Trim the eye of excess fat and slice each eye into four equal noisettes, approximately 1-inch thick. Reserve.

2. Cut each leek into 4-inch lengths, using half white and half green of the leek. Wash thoroughly. Bring 1 quart of water and 3 teaspoons of salt to a boil. Cook the leeks until tender, about 5 minutes. Drain and refresh under cold water. Cut each piece of leek lengthwise into quarters. Reserve.

3. Cut off the base of the artichokes. Trim sides and base until all leaves are removed and the smooth, white base is exposed. Remove choke and scrape center of artichoke bottom. As soon as cuts are made, rub the exposed parts of the artichoke with a lemon quarter to avoid discoloration.

4. Dissolve the flour in 6 cups water in a saucepan. Add 1 teaspoon salt, lemon juice, and artichoke bottoms. Bring to a boil and cook, covered, until artichokes are tender, about 25 minutes. Remove from heat and leave artichokes in the cooking water until ready for use. (*The flour in the water helps keep the vegetable white. Artichokes must be covered with water at all times when cooking.*)

5. Prepare TOMATO CONCASSER. Reserve.

6. Prepare BASIL CREAM SAUCE. Reserve.

7. Fill the artichoke bottoms with TOMATO CONCASSER and place with the leek sections in a casserole. Add the chicken broth and braise in a hot (400°) oven until heated through, about 10 minutes. (*Canned broth is acceptable for braising.*)

8. Heat a thin film of oil in a heavy skillet until very hot. Sprinkle noisettes with salt and pepper on both sides. Sauté to desired doneness, about 1½ minutes on each side for medium rare. Drain noisettes thoroughly on paper toweling because any oil residue will mar the BASIL CREAM SAUCE.

9. Cover the bottom of a warm dinner plate with the BASIL CREAM SAUCE. Place an artichoke bottom filled with TOMATO CONCASSER in the center of the plate. Arrange 4 pieces of braised leek, white part toward the center, around the artichoke like spokes on a wheel. Place 1 noisette of lamb between each leek, 4 on each plate, and serve immediately.

TOMATO CONCASSER

3 medium tomatoes,
   peeled and seeded
1 small clove garlic, finely minced

Salt and pepper to taste
Pinch of sugar

1. Chop the tomatoes very fine or coarse purée in a food processor or blender.
2. In a non-aluminum skillet, cook the tomatoes over moderate heat until almost all of the liquid has evaporated.
3. Add the garlic and sprinkle with salt, pepper, and sugar. Simmer for 3 to 4 minutes. Adjust seasonings. Reserve.

To peel tomatoes, plunge into simmering water for 30 seconds. Peel will slip off easily.

BASIL CREAM SAUCE

2 cups heavy (whipping) cream
   Salt and white pepper to taste
1 teaspoon roux, or as needed*

1 cup loosely packed fresh
   basil, stems removed
¼ cup fresh spinach, blanched
   and shocked in cold water
2 tablespoons butter

1. In a saucepan over medium flame, heat the cream. Add a pinch of salt and white pepper and thicken slightly with roux.

2. Add basil and spinach. Adjust the consistency by adding additional cream if the sauce is too thick to pour easily. Bring to a boil.

3. Remove from the heat and swirl the butter into the sauce. Adjust seasonings.

4. Run through a blender or food processor until the basil and spinach are well incorporated and the sauce is smooth. Strain through a fine sieve.

5. Keep sauce warm until ready to use.

To make a roux, combine equal amounts of flour and butter in a small sauce-pan. Simmer over low heat for 6 to 8 minutes, stirring constantly, or until the flour is cooked. Adjust heat so that the flour does not brown.

A thin film of melted butter spooned on top of the sauce will prevent a "skin" from forming. Stir to incorporate the butter and sauce prior to using.

PROFITEROLES AU CHOCOLAT

12 *small cream puffs*
   (PÂTE À CHOUX)
1 *cup vanilla ice cream*
   (approximately)

½ *cup CHOCOLATE SAUCE*
   Shredded coconut as needed

1. Thinly slice the bottom of each cream puff nearly through to other side (hinge cut) and remove any dough left inside. If the "hinge" breaks, simply replace the entire bottom of the puff in Step 2.

2. Fill the cream puff with ice cream, close the puff, and arrange 3 to a plate.

3. Top each cream puff with CHOCOLATE SAUCE and sprinkle with shredded coconut.

Cream puffs can be made ahead, filled with ice cream, and then frozen. Remove from the freezer a few minutes before serving, then add CHOCOLATE SAUCE and coconut.

THE ROOF

PÂTE À CHOUX

¼ pound butter
¼ teaspoon salt
1 cup water

1 cup flour
3 large eggs, unbeaten

1. Preheat the oven to 375°.
2. Combine the butter, salt, and water in a medium saucepan; bring to a boil.
3. Add the flour all at once. Cook for 1 to 2 minutes, stirring constantly with a wooden spoon until the dough comes loose from the sides of the pan, froms a ball, and then makes a smooth paste. Remove from the heat.
4. Beat in the eggs, one at a time, with the wooden spoon. Be sure each egg is well incorporated into the dough before adding another one.
5. Put the dough into a pastry bag with a 1-inch tip. Pipe out into 2-inch diameter rosettes on a baking sheet covered with parchment paper or lightly greased.
6. Bake at 375° for approximately 30 to 40 minutes.

Makes approximately 18 puffs.

CHOCOLATE SAUCE

8 ounces sweet chocolate
1 cup Hershey's Chocolate Syrup

2 tablespoons rum

1. Combine the sweet chocolate and the chocolate syrup in a double boiler and simmer until the chocolate is melted.
2. Add the rum and combine with the melted chocolate. Keep warm until ready to serve.

Makes 2 cups.

CHOCOLATE SAUCE keeps indefinitely if refrigerated.

RECIPE INDEX

Appetizers

Beverages

Bread, Pasta, and Stuffing

Desserts and Dessert Accents

RECIPE INDEX

RECIPE INDEX

Salads

Salad Dressings

Sauces and Special Seasonings

Soups

RECIPE INDEX

NOTES

DINING IN–THE GREAT CITIES

A Collection of Gourmet Recipes from the Finest Chefs in the Country

Each book contains gourmet recipes for complete meals from the chefs of 21 great restaurants.

____ Dining In–Baltimore $7.95	____ Dining In–Minneapolis/St. Paul, Vol. II . $8.95
____ Dining In–Boston (Revised) 8.95	____ Dining In–Monterey Peninsula 7.95
____ Dining In–Chicago, Vol. II 8.95	____ Dining In–Philadelphia 8.95
____ Dining In–Chicago, Vol. III 8.95	____ Dining In–Phoenix 8.95
____ Dining In–Cleveland 8.95	____ Dining In–Pittsburgh (Revised) 7.95
____ Dining In–Dallas (Revised) 8.95	____ Dining In–Portland 7.95
____ Dining In–Denver 7.95	____ Dining In–St. Louis 7.95
____ Dining In–Hampton Roads 8.95	____ Dining In–Salt Lake City 8.95
____ Dining In–Hawaii 8.95	____ Dining In–San Francisco 8.95
____ Dining In–Houston, Vol. II 7.95	____ Dining In–Seattle, Vol. III 8.95
____ Dining In–Kansas City (Revised) 8.95	____ Dining In–Sun Valley 7.95
____ Dining In–Los Angeles (Revised) 8.95	____ Dining In–Toronto 8.95
____ Dining In–Manhattan 8.95	____ Dining In–Vancouver, B.C. 8.95
____ Dining In–Milwaukee 8.95	____ Dining In–Washington, D.C. 8.95

☐ Check (✔) here if you would like to have a different Dining In–Cookbook sent to you once a month. Payable by MasterCard or VISA. Returnable if not satisfied.

☐ Payment enclosed $_____ (Please include $1.00 postage and handling for each book)

☐ Charge to:

VISA #_____ Exp. Date_____

MasterCard #_____ Exp. Date_____

Signature_____

Name_____

Address_____

City_____ State_____ Zip_____

SHIP TO (if other than name and address above):

Name_____

Address_____

City_____ State_____ Zip_____

PEANUT BUTTER PUBLISHING

911 Western Avenue, Suite 401, Maritime Building ▪ Seattle, WA 98104 ▪ (206) 628-6200